MODERN
B2B MARKETING

*A Practitioner's Guide for
Marketing Excellence*

David E. Sweenor &
Kalyan Ramanathan

It's not the tech that's tiny, just the book!™

TinyTechMedia LLC

Modern B2B Marketing: A Practitioner's Guide to Marketing Excellence

by David E. Sweenor & Kalyan Ramanathan

Published By:

TinyTechMedia LLC

Editor: Taylor Porter
Cover Designer: Josipa Ćaran Šafradin
Proofreader / Indexer: Peter Letzelter-Smith
Typesetter / Layout: Ravi Ramgati
May 2023: First Edition
Revision History for the First Edition
2023-05-23: First Release
ISBN: 979-8-9858227-2-4 (paperback)
ISBN: 979-8-9858227-3-1 (eBook)

www.TinyTechGuides.com

In Praise Of

Mary Kern, Global B2B Technology Marketing Executive

Infused with humor and wisdom gained over decades in marketing enterprise technology, this TinyTechGuide perfectly nails how modern organizations practice B2B marketing. With easy-to-understand models, templates, and practical advice, David and Kalyan break down this well-orchestrated team of marketing specialists to reveal the magic each contributes—individually and, more importantly, collectively—toward the daunting task of successfully taking B2B solutions to market.

Thomas Been, Chief Marketing Officer

This TinyTechGuide is tiny only in format. It's a short read, yet it boasts an incredible amount of knowledge, experience, and, most importantly, common sense. The book, frameworks, and related templates are incredibly useful for marketing leaders, marketing teams, and anyone aspiring to become a better marketer. This is truly a practitioner's guide for marketing excellence!

Shawn Rogers, Marketing Executive, Analytics Thought Leader, and Industry Influencer

TinyTechGuides have quickly built a reputation for delivering highly focused and actionable information in a consumable format. The new Modern B2B Marketing: A Practitioner's Guide for Marketing Excellence *keeps with that tradition. The B2B marketing landscape is evolving quickly and the guide intersects with those changes, providing marketing professionals with a timely and valuable resource.*

Anand Akela, Marketing Executive, CMO, Top-100 Product Marketing Influencer

This TinyTechGuide is a must-read for B2B leaders seeking practical and effective advice on how to build/execute a world-class marketing function. It goes beyond theory and instead provides a wealth of real-world case studies and examples. By emphasizing the importance of a strong marketing team, streamlined processes, and measurable KPIs, this book equips readers with the tools and knowledge needed to succeed in the competitive world of B2B marketing.

Dedication

Dedication from Dave

To my wonderful family—Erin, Andy, and Chris—thank you for your love and support. To mom and dad, for always believing. To Eric and Laura for always being there. To my dog Brady, for barking so much. And lastly, to my friends, colleagues, and network for your support, encouragement, and believing in TinyTechGuides.

Dedication from Kalyan

To my wife, Meera, who encouraged me to write this book. To my kids, Devya and Viveka, who will be surprised to know that their dad can indeed write. To my parents, who always inspired me to do better. And no dedication is complete without a shout-out to our beloved pup Sherlock.

Prologue

TinyTechGuides are designed for practitioners, business leaders, and executives who never seem to have enough time to learn about the latest technology and marketing trends. These guides are meant to be read in an hour or two and focus on the application of technologies in a business, government, or educational setting.

After reading this guide, we hope that you'll have a better understanding of how B2B marketing is applied in the real world—as well as a better idea of how to apply marketing best practices in your business or organization.

Wherever possible, we try to share practical advice and lessons learned over our careers so you can take this learning and transform it into action.

Remember, it's not the tech that's tiny, just the book!™

If you're interested in writing a TinyTechGuide, please visit www.tinytechguides.com.

Table of Contents

CHAPTER 3

CHAPTER 4

CHAPTER 7

CHAPTER 8

Introduction

There are many classes, articles, and books on marketing and specialized functions within marketing—brand marketing, content marketing, social media marketing, influencer marketing, digital marketing, and much more. However, throughout our careers, we have failed to find an adequate, digestible book that explains business-to-business (B2B) marketing organizations in their entirety and how the various parts fit together. We have also not seen many books that go beyond theory and are grounded in day-to-day realities. This book was written to provide practical advice, tips, and best practices on how B2B marketing actually works in real life.

For example, take the development of personas, which are commonly understood to be at the core of many marketing functions. The traditional guidance—endlessly repeated in books and articles—advises you to set up workshops, interviews, and round-table discussions with dozens of prospective buyers and subject matter experts who deeply understand your target personas and what they care about. Now, this is certainly a nice approach, but it's time-consuming and expensive. For most businesses, it's simply not possible, which means many marketing teams have to do the best they can with incomplete information.

The more practical and iterative approach, one we've seen implemented in many companies, goes as follows: start with an educated guess about your persona, look for common buying patterns in your sales and marketing data, talk to your coworkers in sales and customer success about their experiences with customers, and then—finally—build your initial persona. It can be further refined with workshops and other processes; however, with this process, you have a baseline to start marketing with that can be refined over time. Doesn't that sound like a better approach to a complex problem that limits nearly every marketing team and initiative?

In today's complex, fast-paced digital environment, "random acts of marketing" just won't cut it. Rather than picking one specific topic within the marketing function, we've used our combined 50-plus years of experience across 12 different B2B software companies to assemble the only comprehensive guide to modern, B2B enterprise software marketing grounded in day-to-day practice.

Why did we write this book? Everyone who reads this can agree that marketing is irreplaceable to the success of an organization. After all, it is the doorway to building and maintaining relationships with customers. But the last few years have been extremely dynamic, to say the least. First, the world saw unprecedented change due to the COVID-19 pandemic. Customer habits and buying patterns shifted almost instantaneously. COVID accelerated the digital transformation already taking place within organizations, and marketing teams had to adapt overnight—reinventing their customer experience by finding new ways to connect with and engage consumers. At the start of 2023, economic headwinds are shaking up marketing yet again. Finding new go-to-market (GTM) models and customers is now a top priority for every company.

The analyst firm Gartner estimates that companies are increasing marketing spend from 6.4 percent to 9.5 percent of company revenue. Financial services, travel, and high-tech companies are expected to have the largest increases, hovering around 10.4 percent.[1] However, these budget increases could indeed be fleeting. Having been through previous economic downturns, we know that marketing is one of the biggest discretionary areas of spending within a company. If current trends continue, we predict that marketing budgets will shrink.

We may be biased, but we strongly believe marketing teams have undergone a series of head-spinning changes—increased customer demands, shifting enterprise priorities, dwindling resources, and fluctuating budget priorities. Hence, it's even more essential that business leaders, product managers, members of GTM teams, and marketers understand early in their careers how to create a high-performing marketing organization that can meet market demand and fuel company growth. And that's why we've written this book.

Who Is This Book For?

Stakeholders who lead, work, or engage with marketing, including:
- Business leaders and chief marketing officers (CMOs) who want to learn how to build and sustain a high-performing marketing organization.
- Product managers and GTM teams—including sales teams and professionals—who often interact with marketing but don't quite understand how it all fits together.
- Individuals early in their (marketing) careers who want a practical understanding of how B2B software marketing works outside of a classroom setting.

This book is not about marketing technology or a rehash of the Pragmatic Marketing Framework. This book is the practitioner's guide to effective, modern B2B marketing.

What Is B2B Software Marketing?
B2C Marketing

When most people think about marketing, their minds quickly race to business-to-consumer (B2C) marketing. If they don't work in marketing, they probably just think of advertising. It's the most visible part of marketing and everyone sort of understands it.

Whether it's slick car ads, humorous and quirky insurance commercials, promises of wealth from financial services companies and lean physiques from get-fit pitches, or the never-ending onslaught of fast-food come-ons, advertising is pervasive. For the most part, we are inundated with marketing all day, every day. Whether it's television commercials, online ads, digital billboards, or product placement within TV shows and movies, marketing is everywhere. All for the singular purpose of trying to take your dollar. Most of us think we ignore it and that it doesn't influence us. But are we really immune?

To explain this to our friends and family who are not marketing experts, we like to use the analogy of Pepsi versus Coke. If you ask most people what Pepsi and Coke sell, they will generally say soda or soft drinks. But the PepsiCo web page points out that it is the "Global Leader in Convenient Foods and Beverages."[2] In addition to the iconic beverage, PepsiCo has over 500 brands with a portfolio that includes Doritos, Cheetos, Gatorade, Lay's, Mountain Dew, Quaker, and SodaStream. In 2021, it had US$79 billion in net revenue. Although both make food and beverages, we would argue that Pepsi and Coke are closer to brand marketing companies than anything else. Coke outspends Pepsi on advertising almost two-to-one. In 2021, Coca-Cola spent US$193 million while Pepsi spent $114 million on soft drink advertising. "In past years, both companies spent more than a **billion dollars on advertising**."[3] Whether the spending is due to competitive parity or to maintain market share we cannot say. But one thing is certain; we know zero people who drink both Pepsi and Coke. Given a choice, they'll usually prefer one over the other—similar to the McDonald's versus Burger King rivalry. Is that money being wasted? How many people do you know who switch between these two beverages or fast-food companies? Now, we're not B2C marketers, so we'll probably get into some hot soup for the above comments, but we wanted to provide a brief snapshot of B2C marketing.

To summarize, B2C marketing is about:
- Influencing and selling to one consumer at a time.
- Understanding that emotions are as much of a driver as features and functions.

It's also notoriously difficult to measure. Now that we have a perspective on B2C marketing, let's turn our attention to B2B marketing.

B2B Marketing

Compared to B2C, B2B marketing is a totally different game. Rather than trying to influence you to buy something, B2B marketers are trying to convince a business to buy something—and businesses are less susceptible to impulse buying.

Although cars are a big-ticket purchase for consumers, they are low-value items when compared to enterprise software sales that can run, approach, or exceed a million dollars. In B2B marketing, we need to convince a business that it has an issue that needs to be solved today rather than tomorrow. On top of that, it is imperative to convince potential customers that they should use their dollars on our product or service.

Often, marketing and selling to businesses means doing so to a group of people involved in a buying decision. Stakeholders will play different roles, but all of them must be convinced that they 1) have a need, 2) that your solution can solve it in a unique way, and 3) that they must have it now.

This is the enterprise buying process that prospects—often via a buying group—must go through to buy your solution. Marketing in this scenario is **not just creating** white papers, videos, demos, return on investment (ROI) calculators, product tours, best practice guides, buyer guides, and other materials needed to bring the prospect along the process. It must also **deliver** the right content to the right audience at the right time via the right channel. No small feat. It's the reason marketing is such a critical and important part of any company's success.

Table 1.1: B2C vs. B2B Marketing

	B2C Marketing	B2B Marketing
Products	Point products	Multiple products
Customer	One decision-maker	Multiple decision-makers/a buying committee
Targeting	Large sets of consumers	Fewer grouping of customers based on segment/account/persona
Price	Important	Less Important
Time to Purchase	Short	Long
Main Digital Marketing Objective	Website traffic, conversion, and social engagement	Lead generation (although this is slowly changing)
Communication Channel Mix	Disproportionate mix of digital vs. offline channels (almost entirely digital)	Balanced mix of digital vs. offline channels used

Source: Adapted from Innovative B2B Marketing: New Models, Processes, and Theory.[4]

Why Do We Need B2B Software Marketing?

Now that we have a handle on the differences between B2C and B2B marketing, let's examine why we need B2B software marketing.

Without marketing, most B2B products would likely never be discovered. This may be true for B2C marketing as well, but it's more acute for the B2B world. Unlike consumer products, which might be displayed on store shelves or the numerous online storefronts, it's much harder for businesses to "discover" new solutions to their problems on the Internet—unless other businesses make them aware with a finely targeted, holistic marketing strategy. There is little awareness of software brands for people who do not work in that industry. Thus, we need to have an integrated approach to B2B marketing. Key elements of a holistic marketing strategy include:

- **Thought Leadership:** The ability to build trusted content that forms a trusted relationship with your prospective buyers.
- **Demand Generation:** The ability to capture interested-buyer prospects and put them into a sales funnel to convert the prospect into a customer.
- **Sales Enablement:** The ability to make sure the sales team understands the value of your product or services, who the right individuals are to market to, and the target company's business needs.
- **Competitive Differentiation:** The ability to clearly articulate why your product or service is best for the business problem at hand—as opposed to an alternative.
- **Compelling Software:** Not the antiquated software of old but something that is modern, intuitive, and user-friendly.
- **Trusted Brand:** The ability to connect our values to our prospective customers' values.

Now that we have an understanding of the major activities, let's examine the modern marketing mix.

Beyond the 4Ps: The Evolution of the Modern Marketing Mix

When we went to business school, we learned about the 4Ps. Product, place, price, and promotion. Although this was perhaps a useful framework prior to the digital economy, it was primarily centered around the business that was producing the product or service.

- **Product**: Physical goods or services (lots of discussion on the product life cycle).
- **Place**: How to distribute and where customers can buy it.
- **Price**: How much someone is willing to pay.
- **Promotion**: When to offer a sale or discount.

As the Internet evolved and the digital economy grew, the 4Ps framework also evolved. The digital economy is now more customer-centric than ever. In marketing, we have moved from advertising, press releases, inbound sales, and promotions to more customer-centric and experiential marketing.

Organizations now need to deeply understand what B2B buyers want across multiple channels (see Chapter 6). The rise of platforms, partners, hyperscalers (large cloud service providers like Microsoft, AWS, and Google), and ecosystems has also changed the game. As marketers, we now not only need to intimately understand everything about our prospective customers, but we also need to clearly articulate how our offering fits into the broader ecosystem.

A New Model for Marketing, Built Around the Buyer's Journey

The modern marketing organization has many functions, which include:

- Content Marketing
- Brand Marketing
- Demand Generation (aka Demand Gen)
- Product Marketing
- Marketing Operations (aka Marketing Ops, MOPs)
- Customer Advocacy

How do these teams come together to build awareness, generate demand, win new customers, and retain existing ones? Having worked for many years in B2B marketing, we believe that marketing needs to pivot to a new model centered around the buyer's journey. This model puts the buyer at the core of all marketing initiatives and guides all interactions between customers and the business.

The following figure represents this new modern marketing model—the B2B Modern Marketing Framework. This buyer's journey and framework will be a recurring theme throughout this book, so let's look at the various stages of the marketing cycle in more detail.

Figure 1.1: The B2B Modern Marketing Framework

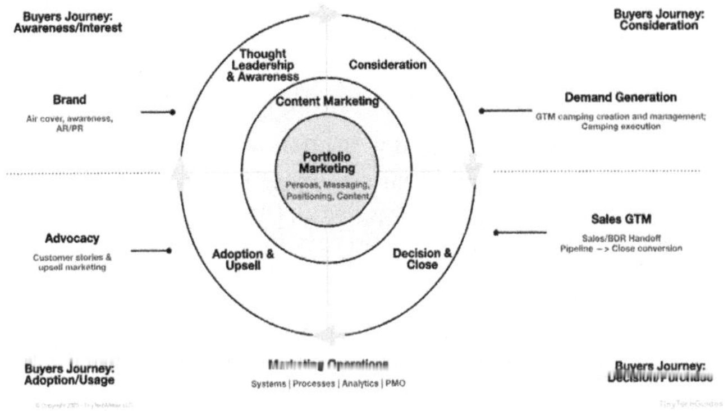

In Figure 1.1 you see the buyer's journey segmented into four stages:

1. **Thought Leadership and Awareness:** Creating brand awareness with your product or service. At this stage, the buyer (singular or group) isn't looking to buy a solution yet, so the goal is to not sell but to inform and educate the buyer about the broad category of problems and solutions the enterprise seeks to solve.

   The corporate marketing and brand team usually takes the lead in this phase of buyer interaction. The prospect may not be ready for the enterprise's product or solution yet; hence, the goal is to make them generally aware of the enterprise's brand and showcase how it can address problems in a unique and differentiated way.

2. **Consideration:** In this stage, the marketing team has generated sufficient interest with the prospect to encourage them to further research your product or solution and interact with your company.

   The integrated campaigns team (aka demand gen) usually leads the interaction at this stage of the buyer journey— providing relevant content and interaction points so buyers can better understand the product and services your organization provides.

9

3. **Decision and Close**: In this stage, the GTM sales team is actively engaged with the buyer through sales motions—demos, proof of concepts, and sales contracts—with the goal being to convert the prospect into a customer.

   The sales team usually leads the interactions at this stage. The product marketing team is also crucial in making sure that the sales team is stage ready—that they have the product and market knowledge, the right content, and competitive materials to help win the customer opportunity.

4. **Adoption and Upsell**: Once the deal closes, the customer starts to use your product or service. Now the marketing team needs to convert this customer into an advocate for your solution so that they can not only sell more products to this customer but use them as a happy referral to bring additional prospects to the company.

   The customer success and advocacy team leads the interactions at this stage. The goal of this team is to showcase the value generated by the product and service from the enterprise so that the customer becomes an active supporter of this solution—providing internal proof for additional expansion and external social proof in the form of testimonials, case studies, etc., that will help convert other prospects to customers.

All four stages are supported by content and messaging led by the portfolio marketing and content teams. The portfolio marketing team provides the core "market intelligence"—information that is usually delivered in the form of content that drives the buyer journey.

And finally, the marketing ops team manages the systems that distribute the content and leads the process of capturing and quantifying the marketing metrics. This ensures that the marketing team is operating efficiently and has the right infrastructure to meet its marketing goals.

As you can see from Figure 1.1, we have mapped each of the major marketing functions within B2B software organizations to this buyer's journey. For marketing to succeed, the entire organization needs to be a well-oiled machine aligned around this buyer's journey. And it is the role of the marketing leader (the CMO) to ensure that the various teams execute their respective functions to support this framework. As you can imagine, getting this all correct is a tall order, which is why this role is a very challenging one.

Bringing It Together Across the GTM Teams

Now that we have an overview of this book, here's a sneak preview of how it all comes together. Marketing does not live in isolation in any company.

The next figure illustrates an integrated approach for how the GTM teams—marketing, sales, and product teams—and their major work streams come together to drive customer engagement and revenue for the company.

Figure 1.2: Major Work Streams for Portfolio, Product, Demand Gen, and Sales Teams

Although this book is primarily focused on the marketing processes within a company, you should keep in mind that both the sales and the product development processes are also extremely important. The three pillars of this golden triangle, if well-aligned, represent an integrated GTM approach.

Practical Advice and Next Steps

High-performing marketing organizations have constant communication and a shared sense of purpose. Achieving this requires the following:

- Defining clearly what you're trying to achieve as a marketing team.
- Understanding what you will need to get it done.
- Defining how to get it done.
- Understanding costs and potential savings for optimization.
- Determining the best organizational structure.
- Defining how performance will be measured.

Summary

In this chapter, we outlined the transformations facing the business world, including new norms and habits from COVID-19, geopolitical instability, and the threat of a global recession. We discussed the current state of marketing budgets and predicted they will likely contract if current trends continue. We then discussed the differences between B2C and B2B marketing.

We've discussed the evolution of the 4Ps and introduced the B2B marketing cycle framework. We then defined a GTM approach that consists of a set of integrated activities spanning product, marketing, and sales functions. If those elements are truly aligned and integrated, they provide the necessary conditions for a high-performing marketing organization.

Chapter 1 References

[1] Turner, Jordan. "What Marketing Budgets Look Like in 2022." Gartner. June 6, 2022. https://www.gartner.com/en/articles/what-marketing-budgets-look-like-in-2022.

[2] PepsiCo. "About PepsiCo." Pepsico. Accessed April 18, 2023. https://www.pepsico.com/who-we-are/about-pepsico.

[3] Paul D. "Coke vs. Pepsi Ads: The Story Behind the Biggest Marketing Rivalry." ContentWriters Blog. October 14, 2022.

https://contentwriters.com/blog/coke-vs-pepsi-the-story-behind-the-biggest-rivalry-in-history/.

[4] Hall, Simon. *Innovative B2B Marketing: New Models, Processes and Theory.* London: Kogan Page, 2022.

CHAPTER 2

Portfolio Marketing

What Is Portfolio Marketing?

For many organizations, portfolio marketing (in many companies also referred to as product marketing) acts as a "glue function" that coordinates GTM activities across product management, sales, presales engineers, marketing, partner ecosystems, and customer success. The next figure illustrates the organizational functions that portfolio marketing interacts with.

Figure 2.1: The "Glue" That Coordinates GTM Activities

Generally, the portfolio marketing team is comprised of subject matter experts (SMEs) who know everything about your product, service, industry, partner ecosystem, or line of business. It is the portfolio marketing team's responsibility to define market segments, identify target personas, dictate messaging, create appropriate content, and train the sales team.

The team leads product launches and often has heavy involvement with developing the corporate pitch deck (the slide presentation your sales team will use to introduce your company and offerings to prospects during sales meetings). It works very closely with corporate marketing/brand teams on thought leadership, integrated campaign teams for demand generation activities, digital marketing teams, and partner marketing teams. It also works with customer success and revenue (sales) enablement teams to ensure the sales teams know how to handle inbound leads.

Figure 2.2: Portfolio Marketing Charter Template

Team Mission: Responsible for understanding markets and buyers to identify new opportunities, develop buyer centric go-to-market strategies, create messaging, launch products and services, and empower sales and partner teams to drive new revenue streams and growth.

Stakeholders		Process Interlocks		Success Metrics	
Marketing • Content • Campaigns/demand gen • Brand & corporate • Customer marekting • Partner marketing **Product** • Product mgmt	**Sales** • Sales mgmt • Revenue enablement • Sales ops **Customer Success** • Customer success mgrs	• GTM strategy • Product launch • Sales & channel strategy • Partner strategy • Campaign planning • Content creation • Revenue (sales) enablement	• Partner enablement • Customer advocacy • Influencer strategy • Pipeline metrics	• Revenue growth • New logo acquisition • Demand gen Performance • Product/marketing/ sales alignment	• Revenue enablement consumption • Pipeline conversion

Market Segmentation	GTM Strategy	Personas & Buyers Journey	Positioning, Messaging, Content	Product Launch	Revenue Enablement
Conduct research and competitive intelligence on competitors. Identify target market segments and potential opportunities.	Partner with product and sales to define and prioritize audience and buyers to grow pipeline more efficiently.	Develop personas and buyer journey maps. Create audience specific messaging, content, and campaigns that will increase conversion rates.	Create positioning and messaging documents for other teams to use to create a consistent market message and GTM strategy.	Create and lead product launch plans for new products in the market.	Create sales enablement material and deliver training sessions to ensure sales knows how to sell your products and services.

Traditionally, portfolio marketing consists of product, solution, industry, technical, ecosystem, and lifecycle marketing. For many businesses, competitive intelligence also sits within the portfolio marketing function, but it's not uncommon to also see it aligned with a product management function. The next figure illustrates a team's charter template for the portfolio marketing function, which you can customize for your specific organization. It contains the team mission, stakeholders, process interlocks, success metrics, and a description of the key activities that the team works on. You can download a copy of the template at TinyTechGuides.com/Templates.

Now that we have a high-level overview of the key activities and what a charter may look like, let's examine each functional area within portfolio marketing in closer detail.

Product Marketing

Product marketing professionals are experts in your product. For organizations with a multitude of products, there is generally one product marketing manager (PMM) for each product with a major revenue stream who acts as a liaison between product management and sales and marketing to articulate the functionality and capabilities of your product.

Industry Marketing

Industry marketing professionals are experts in a particular field, such as banking, finance, insurance, manufacturing, retail, and so forth. They typically have experience working in the field; therefore, they have deep knowledge of the key challenges, problems, and opportunities within the industry. They also have an understanding of the product's capabilities and how it relates to the industry being marketed to.

Solution Marketing

Solution marketing professionals tell the product story across multiple product lines—or the portfolio. The company may have solutions targeting specific industries or lines of business consisting of capabilities spanning multiple products and services. Solutions can be focused on specific industries or a particular line of business, such as human resources, marketing, finance, sales, or operations.

Technical Marketing

Technical marketing managers are typically involved in creating demos, product tours, and multimedia content. Individuals in this role are typically former solution consultants or presales engineers who can have in-depth conversations about the technical capabilities of your product, service, or solution. Many technical marketing managers work across industry, solution, product, and partner ecosystems. They often attend field marketing and third-party events to act as technical subject matter experts.

Partner Ecosystem Marketing

Partner ecosystem marketing managers are responsible for understanding the partner ecosystem to create compelling positioning, messaging, and materials regarding how your product or service, along with a partner's product or service, bring additional benefits to customers. Partnerships could include technology hyperscalers like Amazon, Google, or Microsoft or system integrators like PwC, KPMG, Deloitte, and Accenture.

Competitive Intelligence

Competitive intelligence professionals are responsible for understanding the competition in a particular market or industry. They help the sales team effectively position your organization's products or services relative to competitors and create "battle cards" for the company—one-page summaries of how your product fares against rivals. If the competitive intelligence function reports to the marketing organization, the materials tend to bias toward sales strategies on how to effectively compete. When reporting to the product organization, competitive intelligence materials tend to inform product development, as well as doing more competitive tear-downs to gain an in-depth understanding of the competitors' capabilities.

Why Is Portfolio Marketing Important?

As previously mentioned, the portfolio marketing team acts as a "glue" function that brings together the product, marketing, sales, and customer success organizations. Because of its deep product, persona, and market expertise, it often needs to harmonize differing viewpoints from across the organization. Without a strong portfolio marketing team, the organization risks having inconsistent messaging and a suboptimal GTM strategy. Product launches tend to be lackluster; the organization, as a whole, is often telling inconsistent stories across regions. In the end, the portfolio marketing team needs to provide the company with insights into buying behaviors and changing market conditions. Given the looming threat of inflation, economic uncertainty, and global conflict influencing customer buying decisions, this function is more important than ever.

> As buying behaviors continue to evolve, portfolio marketing can offer unique insight into how buyer behaviors, needs, and preferences are shifting. It can coordinate efforts across the organization to create more compelling, integrated, and valuable buying experiences.

Buying patterns will continue to evolve. The portfolio marketing team needs to understand and adapt to these changing conditions.

Portfolio Marketing Leadership

Fundamentally, the portfolio marketing leader's primary job is to understand the company's business priorities and initiate a formal GTM motion. Portfolio marketing leaders are responsible for the following:

- Creating the GTM strategy in partnership with sales and product teams.
- Clarifying and prioritizing target audiences, growth objectives, organizational structure, sales models, and industry focus.
- Identifying, defining, and evaluating new market opportunities for the company.

19

- Creating a set of processes to align and coordinate how the products, services, and solutions align to different market segments and buyer personas.
- Integrating the prospective perspectives of buyers and customers into the company (customer-centricity is key).
- Leading the product launch process to bring new products into the market.
- Coordinating with sales, technical pre-sales, inside sales, partners, and the broader marketing organization to distribute the content created.
- Acting as the glue between different business units and the corporate marketing function.
- Building a high-performing, marketing team.
- Working closely with revenue (sales) enablement teams to ensure salespeople are well-versed in the company's product, solution, value proposition, and competition.

Now that we know what a portfolio marketing leader does, how is the team typically organized?

Portfolio Marketing Organizational Structure

For larger organizations, a common organizational structure is represented in the following figure.

As illustrated in Figure 2.3, there are four different marketing teams represented: product, solution, industry, and ecosystem marketing. One common challenge occurring with this structure is that it creates artificial silos within the company. For many, the product marketing team may be sending marketing materials to the very same people that the solution or industry marketing teams are targeting. These silos create confusion and friction with prospective buyers, who often receive different messages promoting different products and solutions from the same company.

Figure 2.3: Common Portfolio Marketing Organizational Structure

	Corporate/Brand Marketing					
Product Marketing	Product Marketing (sub-brand)	Solution Marketing (Marketecture)	Solution Marketing (Bundle)	Solution Marketing (Integrated)	Industry Marketing	Ecosystem Marketing
Solution Marketing	Product 1	Product 1	Product 1	Product 1	Product 1	Ecosystem 1
Industry Marketing	Product 2	Product 2	Product 2	Product 2	Solution 2	Ecosystem 2
Ecosystem Marketing	Product 3	Ecosystem 1	Ecosystem 2	Product 3	Ecosystem 3	Ecosystem 3

Source: Adapted from Forrester Research discussions with analyst Rani Salehi.

Perhaps a better approach is to organize your marketing team according to whom you're targeting. As Geoffrey Moore noted in *Crossing the Chasm*, we need to move from product-centric to audience-centric marketing. An example of the difference can be seen in the following table.

Table 2.1: Product vs. Audience-Centric Marketing

Product-Centric Marketing	Audience-Centric Marketing
Easy-to-use	Intuitive and approachable user experience
Sophisticated architecture	Integrates with industry standards
Product price	Whole product price (total cost of ownership)
Unique features	Situational value and fit for purpose

Source: Geoffrey A. Moore, Crossing the Chasm.[1]

If an organization were to realign its marketing organization to an audience-centric alignment, it may look something like what is found in the next figure. For example, in many SaaS marketing organizations, it is common to target users, business leaders, and IT Leaders. And since some of our backgrounds are in data and analytics, we will throw in leaders in this field as well. You could envision an organizational structure where a team of people comes together to create all of the materials required to target a specific audience.

Figure 2.4: Audience-Centric Marketing

	Product Marketing (sub-brand)	Solution Marketing (Marketecture)	Solution Marketing (Bundle)	Solution Marketing (Integrated)	Industry Marketing	Ecosystem Marketing
Audience 1 (IT Leader)	Product 1	Product 1	Product 1	Product 1	Product 1	Ecosystem 1
Audience 2 (Business Leader)	Product 2	Product 2	Product 2	Product 2	Solution 2	Ecosystem 2
Audience 3 (Product User)	Product 3	Ecosystem 1	Ecosystem 2	Product 3	Ecosystem 3	Ecosystem 3

It is the responsibility of the portfolio marketing leader to break down internal organizational silos and move the company toward a buyer-centric approach. In one company, we called this cross-functional group a "pod."

Who Does Portfolio Marketing Report To?

In the B2B software industry, it is common for portfolio marketing to report to either:

1. The marketing leader or CMO.
2. The product leader or chief product officer (CPO).

Although there are various surveys researching this topic, in most high-tech B2B organizations, between 60 percent and 70 percent of portfolio marketing teams report to the CMO. Depending on who the portfolio marketing team reports to, its focus tends to shift.

When the portfolio marketing team reports to the CMO, the key performance indicators (KPIs) and incentives generally align with demand generation activities. Some of these may include thought leadership, analyst relations, and enabling business development reps.

When the portfolio marketing team reports to the CPO, its KPIs and incentives align with the product team's, things like incentives surrounding product management and product launches, product adoption, trials, and early access programs. This approach certainly works well when self-service trials are available, but this approach often limits content creation for the GTM buying process.

What Do Portfolio Marketing Managers Do?

An overview of portfolio marketing activities can be found in this table:

Table 2.2: Portfolio Marketing Activities

Market Segmentation and Sizing	Go-to-Market Approach	Personas and Buyer's Journey Mapping	Positioning, Messaging, and Content Creation	Product Launch	Sales and Revenue Enablement Activities
Market opportunity identification	Target audience identification and prioritization	Identify and define target personas	Create a positioning and messaging framework specific to target personas	Lead product launch processes and coordinate cross-functional activities	Lead training and enablement for sales teams
Market sizing, segmentation, and business plan development	Map portfolio capabilities to buyer needs and pain points	Create persona profiles for target personas	Define benefits and value proposition	Define product launch goals and materials	Work with sales and revenue enablement on scalable training programs
Competitive intelligence	Define and document GTM approach with Product and Sales teams	Understand and document buyer's journey with digital and sales teams	Create personas, messaging, position training, and enablement material for marketing teams	Create product launch plan	Create continual enablement processes for sales teams

Now that we have an understanding of the key activities that a portfolio marketing professional carries out, let's look at the daily responsibilities of a portfolio marketing manager.

A Day in the Life of a Portfolio Marketing Manager

Here are some of the types of meetings, activities, and questions that we—working as portfolio marketers ourselves—have been involved in over the past month.

Go-to-market approach

- Putting together a list of trade shows that we want to attend next year
- Leading efforts to create product naming and packaging for new products.
- Discussing and submitting new product requirements with the product management team.
- Creating themes for events/product launches.
- Participating in several inquiry sessions with industry analysts.

Personas and buyer's journey mapping

- Updating and creating new personas for an existing market opportunity.
- Discussing use cases and needs with prospects and customers.
- Working with customer advocacy to capture new case studies.
- Engaging with the community team on new programs to encourage adoption and usage.

Positioning, messaging, and content creation

- Creating a positioning and messaging framework for a new market opportunity.
- Reviewing event strategy and what messaging should be on a booth for upcoming trade shows.
- Discussing content strategy and writing blogs, scripts, web pages, keynote speeches, press releases, and other market-facing content.
- Planning content for a series of webinars.

- Developing program architecture for an executive-focused event.
- Delivering the keynote speech for an event.
- Creating a new product tour for the company website.
- Working with:
  - The creative team on concepts for new demand generation coming to market.
  - The social media team to create an influencer program.
  - The field marketing team to deliver live and virtual content.
  - The partner marketing team on training and content creation for select partners.
  - The corporate comms team to create content for internal executive comms.
  - Briefing several industry analysts on a new product offering.

Product launch

- Creating a GTM plan for a new product launch.
- Generating content for a new product launch.

Sales and revenue enablement

- Working with the revenue enablement team on sales kickoff (SKO) strategy.
- Creating content for sales kickoff (SKO) strategy.
- Providing SKO content to the sales team.
- Delivering several sales enablement training presentations.
- Engaging with the integrated campaigns team to create Salesloft cadences.
- Working with marketing operations to create new metrics for dashboards.

As you can see, the life of a portfolio marketing team is quite busy and varied.

Whether you are a product, solution, industry, or partner ecosystem marketing professional, there are generally three primary areas of focus: thought leadership, demand generation, and sales enablement. But before any of these can be created, portfolio marketing needs to define the target market segment(s), personas, messaging, and positioning frameworks.

Aspects of Portfolio Marketing

Market Segments

Portfolio marketing managers are responsible for understanding market opportunities. As a part of this, they are often involved and work very closely with product management teams to create a "business plan" for new products. In the end, it is up to portfolio marketing managers to understand the total addressable market (TAM) for their area of focus. What size businesses will be targeted (Fortune 500 or Global 2000)? Is it a goal to go after companies in a specific geographic area? To pursue new logos (businesses) or focus on expansion?

TAM is the size of the market independent of a product or service and is generally used to develop a business case. There are many strategies to calculate a TAM (e.g., number of potential licenses/seats sold or total market value). For companies we have worked for, most calculate TAM using the total market value. This probably stems from the need to raise venture capital funding. To calculate a TAM based on the number of licenses or units, you need to know the number of prospective organizations, the number of buying groups within an organization, and the average size of each opportunity for the number of units.

The market value approach can help to compare different market segment opportunities. To calculate the market value, take the TAM unit count and multiply it by the average selling price (ASP) of each of your units of sale within each buying center.

To recap:
1. Identify the market segment.
2. Identify the segments to be sized (i.e., geography, industry, company size, industry).
3. Identify the number of buying groups.
4. Multiply by the average selling price.

Table 2.3: Illustrative TAM Calculation Example

Market Segments	Number of Companies	Average Number of Demand Units	Average Amount Needed for Buying Group	Total Addressable Market Units	Average Selling Price	Total Addressable Market $
Small Companies	1,000	10	1	10,000	$75,000	$750,000,000
Mid-Size Companies	500	50	5	125,000	$75,000	$9,375,000,000
Large Companies	100	100	10	100,000	$75,000	$7,500,000,000
Total	1,600	160	16	235,000		$17,625,000,000

Personas

Personas are used by the marketing team to identify a common set of challenges and buying behaviors for the target product or service. Much of the literature on personas discusses interviewing potential customers to understand their wants, needs, challenges, and potential opportunities. Additionally, many also suggest that you need to have a persona for each target market or industry.

In practice, this rarely happens. As an example, suppose your company wants to target individuals in a marketing department as well as those in a finance department. Ideally, you would have a specific set of messaging documents for each persona. However, from our experience, most organizations cannot handle more than a handful of personas. What ends up happening is that organizations have a "generic" business leader, IT leader, analytics leader, and other generic user personas rather than having a CMO, chief financial officer (CFO), and user personas for each level.

Figure 3.5: Decision-Making Unit for Enterprise Software Sales

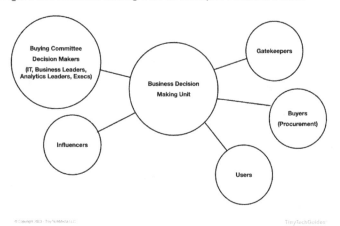

If you think about it, within each of those domains there are multiple sub-functions with different needs. In the CFO organization, you may have leaders and specialists in tax, audit, financial planning and analysis (FP&A), risk and compliance, and so forth. As you can see, targeting each of these personas could quickly become untenable and overly complex for a B2B marketing organization. The next figure represents a decision-making unit for enterprise software sales.

Since B2B marketing involves a decision-making unit rather than an individual buyer, portfolio marketing managers need to think holistically about the buying committee and how best to target them.

Positioning

Positioning is how you frame your product in the context of the market. In *Crossing the Chasm,* Moore explains:

1. Positioning, first and foremost, is a noun, not a verb.
2. Positioning is the single largest influence on the buying decision.
3. Positioning exists in people's heads, not in your words.
4. People are highly resistant to changes in positioning.

The analyst firm Gartner defines positioning as follows:

> An effective positioning statement is the crystallization of your value proposition, differentiated for a specific target audience.[2]

The following table is a common positioning framework adapted from Moore's original work. You can download a copy of the template at TinyTechGuides.com/Templates.

Table 2.4: Positioning Framework Template

Customer Problems	Ideal Solution Framed in Problem Context	Your Answer
For (Target Organization)	Defines the target customer segment for lead generation efforts by marketing and sales and the intended audience for communications and promotions.	Your answer here.
Who Needs (Statement of Need or Opportunity)	Provides the next level of targeting by identifying specific business challenges that the customer is trying to address.	Your answer here.

And Wants (Statement of Experience Expectations)	Define how the company wants to make the customer feel. Depending on where you focus, different aspects of the business could be impacted (e.g., finance/contracts may want an easy licensing approach).	Your answer here.
The (Product/Service Name)	Define the product or service name for your offering.	Your answer here.
Is (Product/Service Category)	Guides the categorization of the solution in the customer's mind.	Your answer here.
That (Compelling Reason to Buy)	Sets the path for most messaging efforts by being the one thing that you want the customers to always remember about the product. Customer service can use this information to help reinforce that value for existing customers during support interactions.	Your answer here.
Unlike (Primary Competitive Alternative)	Sets the competitive landscape, creating a comparison baseline. This helps customers understand not only who you want to be compared to, but also what you could replace. It also impacts your pricing and defines the field on which you compete.	Your answer here.
Our Product (Statement of Primary Differentiation)	This links alternatives to lay out your competitive platform. It should build off your compelling reason to buy, the customer's need, and a unique element for you versus the competition.	Your answer here.

Now that we have a useful template for positioning your product or service offering, let's take a look at messaging.

Messaging

Messaging is a set of materials created to provide a consistent set of descriptions, values, and benefits regarding the product, industry, solution, or partner ecosystem. Ideally, you would have messaging for each persona identified, but this rarely happens in practice. The most important part of messaging is the points of distinction. This is typically a tagline, with three top-line messages, and three sub-bullets for each. It is also typically mutually exclusive, collectively exhaustive (MECE).

An example of a messaging framework can be found in the next figure. You can download a copy of the template at TinyTechGuides.com/Templates.

Pro Tip

It is often a good idea to have your messaging validated by third parties like industry analysts. They bring an external perspective to the table and are often quite helpful in developing strategies to differentiate your products from competitors.

When downloading the template, you will also find benefits and capability mapping, watering holes, persona summary, titles, and more.

Thought Leadership

Portfolio marketing often defines the key themes that a company will discuss from a thought leadership perspective. Leadership will work with the public relations (PR), analyst relations (AR), content, and communications teams to deliver topics to market—whether through blogs, articles, media interviews, whitepapers, and so forth. Thought leadership content provides high-level awareness of the product or service being offered. Portfolio marketing often interfaces heavily with industry analysts like Gartner, Forrester, IDC, and others. We will further discuss this topic in Chapter 5.

Figure 2.6: Messaging Framework Template

<Offering> Messaging Guide> TinyTechGuides™

Elevator Pitch and Points of Distinction

Elevator Pitch:
<e.g. Your Elevator Pitch or Tagline>

Points of Distinction:
< 3 - 5 value based headlines, with three supporting key points; write messages for the different audiences you serve. These should be MECE (mutually exclusive and collectively exhaustive)>

Headline #1
- TBD 1
- TBD 2
- TBD 3

Headline #2
- TBD 1
- TBD 2
- TBD 3

Headline #3
- TBD 1
- TBD 2
- TBD 3

Copy Blocks

(To Be Completed After the Points of Distinction)

5 Word Description

Ciis magnam quibusc iendiore id etur alis ab ipici omnia quaerumquo ese el int eatus iundi dolorecto tem voluptati siti ut quiam exceptam illesequatur modit as aut quam con perovitium erum quunt et repel is dit velluptiora nobitae ligent labor sendi solorro eum dolecus.

25 Word Description

Ciis magnam quibusc iendiore id etur alis ab ipici omnia quaerumquo ese el int eatus iundi dolorecto tem voluptati siti ut quiam exceptam illesequatur modit as aut quam con perovitium erum quunt et repel is dit velluptiora nobitae ligent labor sendi solorro eum dolecus.

4
© 2023 TinyTechMedia | <insert Date> | Version <#> TinyTechGuides

Demand Generation

Portfolio marketing works very closely with the demand generation team (also commonly referred to as campaigns or integrated campaigns team). Portfolio marketers are the subject matter expert for the demand generation team and identify the high-level architecture for the campaigns and sets the content strategy for marketing activities (which includes defining personas and establishing positioning and messaging frameworks). Additionally, they also act as SMEs for campaigns and programs executed by the demand generation function (which will be covered more thoroughly in Chapter 6).

Product Launch

A big portion of the portfolio marketing team's job is to prepare for the product launch. This is one of the most important activities that the company embarks on. The portfolio marketing manager defines and executes the new product introduction (NPI), product launch, and GTM activities, coordinating with any number of other marketing functions. This process includes defining naming, offering, bundle, pricing, packaging, and distribution of the product and services as well as the marketing content /collateral needed to describe the new product to customers, prospective customers, and the broader market.

A sample launch plan template is outlined in the next figure.

Now that we understand all of the activities that comprise the launch plan, how do we measure success? Figure 2.7 represents common launch metrics. It's common for organizations to have different launch tiers, which represent the relative importance and amount of resources your company will invest in the launch. Tier 1 generally represents the highest priority with the most activities, including press releases and analyst pre-briefs, while Tier 3 may simply be a feature enhancement with a simple blog and updated release notes. You can create your own version using the template freely available at TinyTechGuides.com/Templates.

Figure 2.7: Sample Launch Plan Template

How do you measure success? This will certainly vary by company, but we have included common launch metrics in the next figure by tier across three dimensions—business performance, marketing effectiveness, and sales enablement.

Figure 2.8: Common Product Launch Metrics by Launch Tier

	Offering or Segment Performance	Marketing and Sales Effectiveness
Business Impact	• Revenue • Licenses sold • Sales pipeline • Market share • Penetrate rate • Win / loss ration • New logos	• Response rates/engagement • Campaign performance • Cost per sales qualified lead (SQL) • Influencer share of voice (SOV) • Campaign effectiveness/ROI • Trial Rates
Portfolio Team Output	• Revenue • Licenses sold • Sales pipeline • Attach rate • Account growth • Average deal size	• Response rates/engagement • Campaign performance • Cost per sales qualified lead (SQL) • Influencer SOV • Campaign effectiveness/ROI • Trial rates
Portfolio Team Activities	• Retention rate • Upgrade rate • Pipeline volume	• Feature trial • Feature utilization

Now that we understand the product launch process and associated metrics, let's look at brand and special projects.

Brand and Special Projects

The portfolio marketing team is also commonly involved in special projects such as creating corporate messaging and positioning, the corporate deck, and other high-value, special projects. Whether you are building total cost of ownership (TCO) or ROI calculators for the website or creating product tours, the portfolio marketing team is generally at the center of these activities. These projects are typically cross-functional and take a significant amount of time to achieve alignment. Portfolio marketing is also heavily involved in mergers and acquisitions.

Pricing and Packaging

Since portfolio marketers' job is to be audience-centric, they often work with product and competitive intelligence teams to ensure that their offering is competitive. They help define pricing, bundling, and distribution strategies.

Who Makes the Best Portfolio Marketers?

In our careers, we have worked with some fantastic portfolio marketing managers. Attributes that are common among some of the best are:

- Domain expertise
- Science, technology, engineering, and math (STEM) backgrounds
- Curious and innovative
- Continual learners
- Barrier removers
- Communicators
- Proactive
- Empathetic

David's set of guiding principles are as follows:

- Produce something, rather than nothing.
- Whatever you do, be impactful.
- Have fun while doing it.
- Think big, start small, act fast.

And Kalyan's guiding principles are similar:

- Clarity through action!
- A good plan executed today is far better than a perfect plan executed next week.

- You miss every shot not taken (take risks, lots of them).
- Passion, skill, knowledge (in that sequence).
- Learn every day—you are always a white belt.

We will come back to this in Chapter 9.

How to Measure Portfolio Marketing Success?

Metrics for portfolio marketing managers are often quite tricky. Since the they are the "glue function," they typically don't "own" the specific KPIs. They:

- Work with brands but don't "own" the awareness metrics.
- Work with public relations but don't "own" the media placement strategy and metrics.
- Work with analyst relations but don't "own" the AR metrics.
- Work with demand generation but don't "own" the pipeline numbers.
- Work with digital teams but don't "own" the digital metrics.
- Work with sales but don't "own" the revenue target.
- Work with customer success managers but are not responsible for retention.

Defining success is quite squishy. For most marketing organizations, there is a maniacal focus on pipeline generation—as this leads directly to revenue. The portfolio marketing team can look at consumption metrics for non-gated or unattributed activities such as thought leadership, social media, and other activities.

Another qualitative but important measure of product marketing manager (PMM) success is the influence and impact you have on sales—sales training, sales enablement, and sales opportunities. The more PMMs engage with sales and are seen as influential in accelerating opportunities and deals, the better!

The analyst firm Forrester suggests linking actions to goals. It developed the framework that is the basis of the following table.

Table 2.5: Linking Actions to Goals

Action Types	Measure
Impact: Effects against business goals	• Revenue where thought leadership impacted • Market share • Profit • New logos • Retention rates and advocacy • Customer engagement
Output: Direct results of action	• Personas completed • Sales content usage • Product launch • Trials • Assets downloaded • Analyst and media placements • External speaking engagements • Percentage of thought leadership materials
Activity: Counts of action	• Persona interviews • Persona cards • Messaging docs • Sales cards • Cheat sheets • Competitive battle cards • Thought leadership pieces • Analysts briefed
Readiness: Preparedness to perform	• Sales certifications • Personas deployed • GTM validation • Number of SMEs and writers • Influencers engaged

Source: Adapted from Forrester Research discussions with analyst Rani Salehi.

A quarterly business review (QBR) framework is also defined, as seen in the next figure.

Figure 2.9: Portfolio Marketing QBR Framework

Practical Advice and Next Steps

- Create a strong portfolio marketing function —it will act as the glue and ringmaster for many activities within the organization.
- Go through the rigor of creating tight messaging, positioning, and personas —although it can be a slog, this will save work in the long run.
- Form cross-functional relationships with sales, pre-sales, and the CSM teams.

Summary

In this chapter, we learned that portfolio marketing:
- Is the "glue" in many organizations (we have provided a portfolio marketing team charter template).
- Is responsible for coordinating the GTM activities across sales, marketing, product, and customer service teams.
- Creates market segmentation, personas, messaging, and sales enablement material.

- And that KPIs and metrics are often not concrete, but we have provided a framework for how to think about a QBR for a portfolio marketing team.

Chapter 2 References

[1] Moore, Geoffrey A. *Crossing the Chasm: Marketing and Selling Disruptive Products to Mainstream Customers.* 3rd ed. New York: Collins Business Essentials, 2014.

[2] Antin, Alan, Michael Maziarka, and Molly Beams. "Positioning Revisited." Gartner. September 15, 2020. https://www.gartner.com/en/documents/3990177.

Brand Identity and Corporate Marketing

What Is a Brand and Why Does It Matter in B2B Marketing?

While brand marketing is perhaps most associated with B2C marketing (remember the Pepsi and Coke example in Chapter 1?), brand marketing is equally important in B2B marketing. It is perhaps best thought of as the marketing of a company's reputation in relation to the other companies' reputations (in its market categories as well as those of peers in adjacent markets). This is important for several reasons, which we will describe shortly. However, one of them is the commoditization of B2B software, i.e., B2B software becoming more commonplace. Once a customer, prospect, influencer, or even (perhaps especially) an employee or potential employee understands that a certain set of solutions are essentially equivalent, the next most important factor driving a purchasing decision is the reputation or brand of that company.

Today, over 60% of consumers look for brands they can trust before they look at price. And their definition of trust has shifted; they expect brands to take an active stand on the issues that matter to them, while the products solve everyday problems. The tried-and-true emotional and aspirational drivers like image and status are taking a backseat to health, family, quality and social responsibility.[1]

Beyond factors like features, price, and service, it is the **reputation of the brand**—what it stands for, what it cares about (values), what it promises, how unique those promises are, and how reliably it delivers on these—is what separates the winners from the losers. Simon Sinek calls this the WHY of a company— what your company does and how the company does it fall in the domain of the portfolio marketing team, but conveying *why* you do it and why someone should care is the bread and butter of brand marketers.

The clearest and most time-tested example of the power and importance of managing a company's brand is probably Apple. It is a company renowned for how it has, over the years, established and maintained its brand image and reputation. For all intents and purposes, the iPhone is equivalent to and, on certain features inferior to, an Android phone. It's the brand that has become the tiebreaker and allows Apple to charge a premium for its products and services.

A brand is an abstract concept that helps prospective buyers identify a company or product. A brand identity is an interconnected set of visual elements—like logos, colors, fonts, a company description, and other creative elements— that distinguish your brand in the minds of consumers.

We had the opportunity to discuss what a brand means with Darrin Shimizu, who has served as a vice president of marketing, creative, brand, and event production for large B2B technology companies. He said:

> A brand should clearly explain what it represents, both visually and in the message. A brand should clearly stand for the values and benefits it represents, be consistent in every usage, and inspire the people who represent the brand.

Why Is Brand Marketing Important to a B2B Software Organization?

According to Shimizu, what is vital is that:

> The brand embodies the identity of what it represents. If you don't invest in your brand, you can't have a consistent message about what the brand represents. The investment doesn't have to be all of your marketing budget; the investment needs to be a consistent effort to create a strong, clear, and inspiring brand, and making sure everyone who presents the brand, buys into the consistency of it.

Although most of the research on customer loyalty and affinity to purchase is in the B2C space, there is a growing body of commentary and research that suggests that branding is just as important for B2B software companies. We especially see an increased interest and emphasis from B2B software organizations on social issues like environment, social, and governance (ESG) and diversity, equity, and inclusion (DEI).

Below are three reasons why you should invest in brand marketing:

1. **Differentiation**: You need to set both your company and your company's solution apart from the competition. *Both* are important to win customers today. A successful brand identity conveys why (you should care), what (you do differently), and how (you do it better).

2. **Attract and Retain Employees**: Gen Z and millennials make up 46 percent of the U.S. workforce. They care more

about social issues than previous generations and want to believe in what a company stands for, not just how much revenue a company makes.

3. **Shared Values**: Both consumers and employees have more choices than ever and want to work for, and buy from, companies with shared values that consistently and authentically communicate those values.

Let's examine each one of these three points below.

Setting Yourself Apart from the Competition

In the mind of many B2B buyers, the features and functions of enterprise software are becoming a commodity. In other words, most of the capabilities across various software packages in the same market are undifferentiated. A study by the *Harvard Business Review* identified 40 elements of value important to customers that a company can use to help differentiate itself in a market. These factors have nothing to do with the product a company sells.[2] This is illustrated in the next figure.

Figure 3.1: Sources of Value

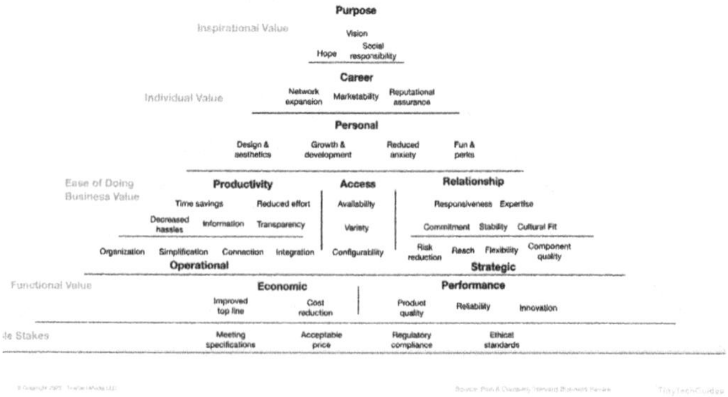

Source: Adapted from "The B2B Elements of Value," [original source Bain & Company], Harvard Business Review.[3]

We will not discuss this in detail, but it is conceptually similar to Maslov's Hierarchy of Needs. At the bottom of the pyramid, we have table stakes and functional (think product) sources of value. Once these needs are met, we move toward sources of value that become less related to the product and more personal. We move from the ease of doing business value (i.e., time savings) to individual value (e.g., personal and career-related) and, finally, to inspirational value (e.g., purpose, social responsibility, and hope). These are the exact value drivers that are being exposed by Gen Z and millennial buyers.

So, which ones are most important? The next figure highlights the importance of these factors for IT infrastructure buyers.[4] The first three elements (product quality, expertise, and responsiveness) lie within the first three sections of the value pyramid and relate to the product and ease of doing business, falling within the functional and ease of doing business value. The remaining seven items fall in the top two sections of the pyramid in the individual and inspirational value sections.

Figure 3.2: Importance-Factor Ratings for
IT Infrastructure Buyers

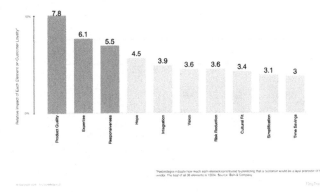

Source: "The B2B Elements of Value," [original source Bain & Company], Harvard Business Review.[5]

Fundamentally, the software industry has matured to the point where everything generally works as designed and meets the functional needs of the group. The responsibility of the brand team is to highlight these differentiating factors of value.

To further illustrate that software is increasingly commoditized, let's look at the customer relationship management (CRM) software market.

Here's how the popular software review website G2 defines CRM software:

> CRM (customer relationship management) software tracks and manages customer relationships. It records interactions between a business, its prospects, and its existing customers. CRM software products place all relevant customer data like contact information, history, and transaction summaries into a concise live record.[6]

G2 has created the G2 Grid® to compare vendors in many different markets. For the CRM market, we can see 812 listings of different software packages, as illustrated in the next figure![7]

Figure 3.3: G2 Grid® CRM Software Market

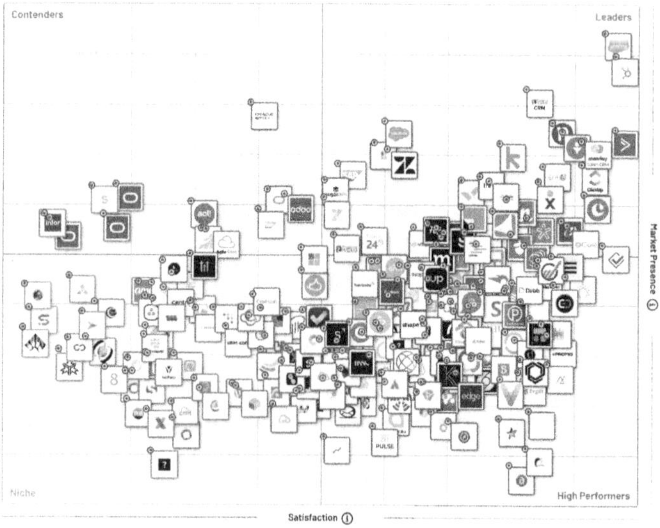

Source: "Best CRM Software," G2.[8]

Given that there are 812 software packages in this one market alone, how do you choose one to buy?

Social Responsibility: The Growing Influence of Gen Z and Millennials

The second reason why it's important to invest in brand marketing relates to the shifting population dynamic and the importance that younger generations are placing on social issues. Not only will millennials and Gen Z (who currently make up 46 percent of the U.S. workforce) become a greater portion of our employee base, but they will also gain more influence and say in corporate purchase decisions. This dynamic will make the investment and promotion of brands more important than ever for B2B software companies.

> 72% of your buyers say they are more likely to buy from socially responsible businesses, according to a recent survey. That's 17 points higher than the general public.[9]

A strong brand offers your company a face that potential consumers will recognize when making purchasing decisions, which can convert one-time buyers into loyal, repeat customers. A good brand may help a firm stand out from its competition, boost its market position, raise revenue, and much more.

Branding will increase client trust in you. When someone wants to purchase an item or use a service, they will go with a firm that has an established brand reputation and personality that they like. Building trust can be difficult initially, especially if your company is new to the market and few people are familiar with it.

As purchasing power transfers from older to younger generations, brand trust is becoming increasingly important for businesses. Working and associating with firms they trust—companies whose brands are portrayed openly and honestly and that align with their values—is most important to Millennial and Gen Z customers.[10]

Shared Values: Employees and Consumers Have More Choice Than Ever

The third factor why branding is important for companies to invest in is related to both employee and customer choice. Given the relatively low switching costs for prospective customers and employees, a strong brand with shared values will lead to greater satisfaction, profitability, and retention.

An increasingly important and visible part of the brand narrative is a company's stance on social and environmental issues. Whether it's DEI or ESG, a brand must be thoughtful and active in how it manages and communicates its stance on a myriad of issues. The analyst firm Forrester stated:

The days when B2B companies could remain silent on important social issues are over. Organizations are increasingly judged by how they act on issues ranging from diversity and inclusion to immigration and vaccine mandates. When faced with this level of scrutiny, many B2B brands are ill-prepared to face this challenge. In Forrester's 2020 Brand And Communications Survey, 52% of marketing leaders did not have a fully defined brand purpose, which sets a course for social action and corporate social responsibility. Yet these same organizations understand that brand purpose is important to new buyers (82%), employees (63%), and market influencers (64%).[11]

> **Pro Tip**
>
> Marketing leaders need to ensure the company's executive team is having active discussions not only on what the HR position is on a variety of DEI and social issues but also on what the internal and external communication strategies will be regarding those issues. Ensuring a well-vetted crisis communication process with clear roles, responsibilities, and decision trees is vital to managing a brand's reputation.

Lastly, "Building a brand that attracts and retains talent—employer branding—is at the top of the C-Suite agenda and is the most critical priority among CMOs, according to a 2022

Forrester CMO Pulse Survey."[12] Retention is more difficult than ever, and attracting talent through strong DEI initiatives can be a game-changer in terms of talent acquisition, retention, and performance.

Now that we have hopefully convinced you of the importance of brand marketing, what do brand and corporate marketing do exactly?

What Do Brand Marketers Actually Do?

Brand marketing teams are typically comprised of creative teams that both design and write content, but also, importantly, should include brand strategists and program managers. There's a good deal of "head" or science work that should proceed the "heart" or artwork of the brand. These are two sides of the same coin—head and heart or science and art, whichever way you want to think about it.

Brand strategy is based on the DNA of the company. For instance, is it product-led, sales-led, or customer-led? What market and target audience is it trying to serve and appeal to, what are the company's and the solution's true differentiators, and why should people believe and care about what your brand is projecting? These are all important elements of a brand and should be foundational to developing the heart/art part of the brand—its logo, color palette, imagery, tone, voice, etc.

An important strategic element of brand strategy is who your brand is trying to appeal to and where you find more of those people so you can grow your brand awareness. Unless you're one of the big three (Apple, Microsoft, or Amazon), you need more people to become aware of your brand—the solutions it provides and why these matter. Developing an awareness plan and program that includes some mix of advertising (mostly digital but also traditional TV, streaming TV, billboards, etc.), social media, and events are a central part of managing a brand. These channels of awareness are often referred to as the "paid" channels since varying budgets are required to utilize them.

That is not to say that the creative (design and content) aspects of brand marketing should be underestimated. At the end of the day, everything your company/brand wants to communicate to its audience needs to come across with words and pictures. Whether it's a highly visible keynote presentation by your CEO, your website, or your content and collateral, writers and designers need to produce work in a way that is compelling, actionable, and in sync with the brand image.

> **Pro Tip**
>
> Often, creative teams are at the end of the food chain of ideation, planning, and creation. Include your creative team early in the planning of new content, campaigns, and events. Rich, compelling creative design and writing can be the differentiator in how effective a brand is in conveying its unique value.

Brand and Demand: Friends or Foes?

It's thought that these two functions compete for the same dollars and organizational focus, creating a broad misconception that there needs to be a focus on one or the other—brand or demand. However, in most organizations, quite the opposite is true. Demand marketing leaders worth their salt want as much brand awareness marketing as their organization can afford. They know that the more the brand is known to prospective buyers that are potential leads or opportunities, the easier and cheaper they are to acquire. And any experienced brand marketing leader knows that the BEST way to validate the importance and success of brand marketing efforts is a growing funnel of leads and a sales pipeline.

It's also true that demand marketing teams require a range of "shared services" from the brand or corporate marketing teams. Those include:

- Brand guidelines and creative services, including the creation of compelling campaigns.
- Content, content, content. Demand gen teams build all

their programs and tactics around delivering content offers that prospects will be interested in.

- Brand awareness programs, digital and otherwise, which increase interest at the top of the funnel so that demand gen offers can nurture these prospects into qualified leads and, ultimately, sales opportunities faster and more effectively.

What is the balance from a budget perspective? A common rule of thumb is the 60/40 rule which states that 60 percent of the budget should be spent on brand campaigns and 40 percent of the budget on activations (an event, campaign, or experience that builds brand awareness). However, from our experience, we see this closer to 50/50 or skewed the other way to 40/60.

Now that we understand that brand and demand are complementary and not adversarial, let's look at what a brand marketing manager does.

A Day in the Life of a Brand Marketing Manager

As described previously, "brand marketing" roles include strategists, program managers, designers, and writers. The day-to-day activities of these professionals include:

- Establishing a corporate brand strategy.
- Ensuring that the brand identity is compelling and executed consistently.
- Creating compelling campaign visuals that capture the target audience's attention.
- Making sure the brand is represented properly in all new marketing material.
- Working with the portfolio marketing team on establishing the corporate message.
- Partnering with digital marketing teams on advertising and the creative treatment of ads.

- Establishing brand guidelines:
  - These include standardized visual and voice elements that make up the brand identity, which need to be applied consistently.
  - Elements that are appropriate for both offline (collateral, events) and online (web, social, digital marketing, presentations, etc.) environments.
  - Material should be global in nature and include, if necessary, where and how geographical discretion should be applied.
- Working with the web team to create compelling web experiences.
- Creating concepts and producing a multitude of creative assets, including campaign material, digital and print ads, videos, collateral, web pages and websites, presentations, event materials, etc.
- Defining an effective outsourcing model and managing agencies for quality outcomes and cost-effective budgets.
- Securing easy-to-use PowerPoint templates and layouts for the organization to use.
- Ensuring Canva and other templates are available for sales and marketing teams to use.
- Authenticating that the brand is brought to life at corporate events.
- Cooperating with corporate sponsorships and partners to develop co-branding strategies.
- Creating any number of brand identity elements for employees to use, including email signatures, social media templates, banners, and other branded items.
- Managing a company swag store to efficiently and cost-effectively provide branded items for employees and customers.
- Working with partners to create co-brands for marketing teams to use.

This is just a partial list. In the end, these folks are highly creative, collaborative, and engaged with many of the different marketing functions.

Corporate Sponsorships

In many organizations, brand marketing is also responsible for corporate sponsorships. In B2B software marketing, football (both kinds), baseball, basketball, golf, tennis, Formula 1, and other sports are often popular sponsorships. Although the research on the ROI of sports marketing is mixed, companies are spending lots of money in this area.

From our experience, most of these sponsorships arise because specific individuals (i.e., executives) within a company are fans of a particular sport and have a personal interest in attending events or enjoy being associated with the sport or a particular brand within it. The sales team loves them as well. However, if you're bringing your best customers to these events, will that be the tipping point for closing the deal? Or would the deal have closed anyway? What we found is that the executives we discussed this with all said that corporate sponsorships definitely increased brand awareness!

Who Makes the Best Brand Marketers?

I asked Darrin Shimizu this question. He provided some qualities and attributes that he looks for when hiring brand, creative, and corporate marketers:

- **Creative**: Stating the obvious, but successful brand marketers need to be able to look at things both within their current brand and style and also at new trends, understanding what people with different knowledge bases bring to a project and how to be creative about everything.
- **Collaborator**: Brand marketers need to be able to work with people, compromise with them, help them see their vision, and treat individual projects and people in their own unique ways. They don't consider themselves the "brand police." Rather, they consider themselves "brand ambassadors," ready to be creative and collaborative in service of the brand.

- **Communicator**: Same as above, which involves understanding the importance of communicating an idea, listening to someone else's idea, and either finding a compromise or being able to clearly explain why something will or won't work.
- **Team Player**: Most brand marketers and corporate markers are part of a larger organization and work with people in many different areas at various levels of the institution. Learning how to navigate that is critical.
- **Problem Solver**: We're faced with so many issues that often come from multiple angles. Brand managers need to be able to prioritize problems and come up with ways to solve them, either on their own or by knowing when to ask for help.
- **Possess Strong Time-Management Skills**: Most members of a creative team will be left on their own to work on projects. Being able to properly account for one's time and prioritize projects to stay on deadline is critical.

Now that we have an understanding of who makes the best brand marketers, let's look at some KPIs.

KPIs for Brand Marketing

As mentioned in the previous section, it is often harder to measure brand marketing effectiveness since it is a long-term strategy. A survey by BCG, which looked at the primary reasons organizations were investing less than 20 percent of their budget on brand activities, found that:
- Brand marketing has a business impact, but companies were **unable to measure it**.
- **Key stakeholders didn't believe** in the business impact of brand marketing.
- There was a lack of **capabilities** to successfully market brands, e.g., lack of cohesive messaging.[13]

A very common question, up and down an organization, is "How do you measure brand?" It's a good but, unfortunately, not straightforward question. Over the years, we've come to accept that there are no metrics that measure the impact of the brand. Instead, our collective wisdom says that a range of KPIs is the best approach. Common brand KPIs include:

- **Increased quality visits to your website over time**. There are many different metrics gleaned from a website, but seeing that—quarter over quarter—more people in your target audience are coming to your website and engaging with your content is an indication that awareness tactics are working.
- **Increased engagement with content** on your website and via third-party channels.
- **Social media followership and engagement growing** quarter over quarter. It's important to measure both followership and engagement. You don't want to add a bunch of new users who are not engaging with your content.
- **Healthy and growing attendance** to your large marquee events.
- **Positive third-party analyst reviews** and reports.
- **Increased media share of voice (SOV)**, which is the amount of coverage your company receives compared to a group of competitors or peers.
- **Increased pipeline of leads, opportunities, and revenue**. While the brand team is not directly responsible for these metrics, if it isn't moving up and to the right over time, then brand marketing efforts can't be deemed successful. More inquiries and leads at the top of the funnel are likely more attributable to brand awareness efforts.

How Are Brand and Corporate Marketing Related?

As organizations grow—typically north of $300 million annual recurring revenue (ARR)—bringing several brand and "comms" functions together is often pursued (corporate communications will be discussed in Chapter 4). This helps increase the synergy between several functions that have brand communication in common *and* it helps the CMO avoid too many siloed, direct reports! These functions often include some combination of:

- **Brand Marketing:** Strategy, awareness or paid programs, and creative.
- **Corporate Communications**: PR/media, analyst relations, executive communications, and increasingly internal communications and social media.
- **Content Marketing and Thought Leadership**: Working closely with portfolio marketing on content. To ensure the right content is getting to the right audiences via the right channels, content marketing works closely with the creative team to package on-brand content in attractive, compelling ways.
- **Strategic Event Marketing:** There can be no better way to loudly and proudly project your company's brand than through a major customer or trade show event. Having the events team in close proximity to the brand and creative teams can be very helpful and impactful.
- **Web and Digital**: A company's website and social media are considered the "owned" channels, where you drive and own the delivery of the message; you don't have to pay others to use them. In some cases, the website and overall digital marketing program are owned by demand generation teams. Even so—especially so—it's vital that there is tight alignment with the company's brand and digital properties. Regardless of where the website and digital marketing programs sit organizationally, the brand must be delivered consistently. Today, there is no more important brand platform than a company's website and social media channels.

Practical Advice and Next Steps

- A brand is ever-evolving. Think carefully about what your brand represents and how you orchestrate multiple functions to deliver a compelling and consistent brand experience.

- As buying habits change, you will need to use the brand hierarchy pyramid to represent your brand with values that align with personal and aspirational values.
- Create a measurement program and establish a robust set of KPIs to measure the impact of your brand. Be proactive in this area. Don't wait for key stakeholders to question the impact of marketing the brand.

Summary

- Brand marketing is the creative engine within the organization; it is important to have a well-articulated brand strategy and to execute it creatively and consistently.
- As demographics shift, millennials and Gen Z will have increased buying power; their attitudes and preferences are different from baby boomers and Gen X.
- Organizations will need to pay more attention to their brand as software functionality is commoditized.
  - There is a tangible ROI on brand activities.

Chapter 3 References

[1] Murtell, Jennifer. "Does the World Really Need More Brands?" American Marketing Association. April 11, 2022. https://www.ama.org/marketing-news/does-the-world-really-need-more-brands/.

[2] Almquist, Eric, Jamie Cleghorn, and Lori Sherer. "The B2B Elements of Value." *Harvard Business Review.* March–April 2018. https://hbr.org/2018/03/the-b2b-elements-of-value.

[3] Almquist, Cleghorn, and Sherer. "The B2B Elements of Value."

[4] Almquist, Cleghorn, and Sherer. "The B2B Elements of Value."

[5] Almquist, Cleghorn, and Sherer. "The B2B Elements of Value."

[6] "Best CRM Software." G2. Accessed December 24, 2022. https://www.g2.com/categories/crm.

[7] "Best CRM Software." G2.

[8] "Best CRM Software." G2.

[9] Hoffman, Constantine von. "B2B Buyers Are Much More

Concerned about a Company's Values than the General Public." MarTech. August 11, 2022. https://martech.org/b2b-buyers-are-much-more-concerned-about-a-companys-values-than-the-general-public/.

[10] Heyward, Chastity. "Why Branding Your Business Is Important in 2022." *Forbes.* June 16, 2022. https://www.forbes.com/sites/forbesbusinesscouncil/2022/06/16/why-branding-your-business-is-important-in-2022/?sh=5dfd92952cb2.

[11] Bruce, Ian, and Lori Wizdo. "Envisioning Powerful B2B Brands Drives Long-Term Value Creation." Forrester. January 18, 2022. https://www.forrester.com/report/envisioning-powerful-b2b-brands-drives-long-term-value-creation/RES176937.

[12] Chatterjee, Dipanjan, Melissa Bongarzone, and Alex Schanne. "Employer Branding Is the New Marketing Imperative." *MIT Sloan Management Review.* July 21, 2022. https://sloanreview.mit.edu/article/employer-branding-is-the-new-marketing-imperative/.

[13] Sheerin, Alannah, Peter Dewey, David Ratajczak, Mary Katerman, and Tim Rice. "Why B2B Brand Marketing Matters." BCG Global. November 9, 2021. https://www.bcg.com/publications/2021/why-brand-marketing-matters.

CHAPTER 4

Corporate Communications

What Are Corporate Communications?

As mentioned in Chapter 3, buying patterns are changing as more Zoomers (Gen Z) and millennials gain decision-making authority within organizations. These are sophisticated buyers, born in the digital age, who increasingly buy from companies that have values that align with their own—especially when it comes to ESG and DEI topics. These new buyers expect companies to take a stance on social justice issues, whether it be Black Lives Matter, immigration, or trade policies.

According to the 2022 Edelman Trust Barometer, 58 percent of survey respondents buy or advocate for brands based on their beliefs and values, and 60 percent chose a place to work based on their values and beliefs.[1] Organizations can no longer sit back and watch from afar when some societal event happens—they need to be ready to take a stance and make sure that both current and prospective customers understand the company's values and positions on the relevant topics, and likewise with employees. This is the responsibility of the corporate communications team (also referred to as corporate comms).

Corporate communications are the megaphone for the brand reputation we described earlier. This function includes all the various ways the key elements of a brand are communicated to a variety of audiences—the media, industry analysts, customers, partners, and current and prospective employees. If successful, your message will find its way into influential mediums that are seen as unbiased—prominent business press, trade publications, analysts' reports, rating sites, and so forth. These channels are often referred to as earned media because, as previously mentioned, you earn your way into coverage versus buying it.

Effective communication is critical for every organization. It's the bedrock that defines how a company represents itself to the market. Corporate comms informs:

- Customers and prospects about a company's products or services and its unique value compared to competitors.
- Investors, the media, and the general public about important organizational developments.
- Internal employees who can use the company's communication and messages to coordinate activities.

It's not surprising that most organizations will eventually realize they need to invest in building a strong corporate communications team responsible for these various activities. The role of the comms team is to help guide the company, elevate and amplify its messages, and generate awareness and impact. Essentially, corporate comms needs to create a compelling, differentiated, and engaging communications platform that establishes the enterprise—and its leadership team—as a category definer and thought leader.

Why Are Corporate Communications Important?

As mentioned in previous sections, customers and prospects buy from companies that establish trustworthy brands aligning with their values and beliefs. If a company loses this trust and positive brand perception, prospective buyers will shop elsewhere. It may take years for the company to build up brand loyalty.

It's important to communicate with customers in a way that promotes brand awareness, reinforces the brand image, builds press relations, and ultimately grows businesses. The corporate comms team within organizations helps to define a strategy and consistent tone of voice for the organization's internal and external communications.

Corporate comms help to communicate the company's mission and values and information about products and services, in addition to addressing any issues, concerns, or crises that may arise. Besides building trust and credibility among stakeholders, effective corporate communications can also lead to greater business opportunities for a B2B company by helping it develop a competitive advantage over its competitors.

For example, what if your company has a layoff or corporate restructuring? What if there is a data breach? What if there is a key social issue that needs to be addressed? How do you communicate your biggest product launch of the year? What if you brought on a new world-class leader to the C-Suite? It's the corporate comms team that coordinates the public perception of all such instances. Especially important to success is how the company responds to crises.

Corporate Comms in Action

In 2022, many software technology companies were hit with a Log4j vulnerability, which affected nearly every technology company (along with hundreds of millions of devices). Log4j is an open-source software package used by most software products; a patch was needed to mitigate this vulnerability. While many software companies were able to quickly release updated software to customers with the right fixes (or suggest an alternate way to handle the issue), companies with well-oiled communication strategies were able to capitalize on this issue even more and make it a true selling point. Such companies tried a variety of tactics:

- Public communication and blogs to instantly highlight how to fix their software.
- Best practices to remediate general issues for customers (how to track usage of Log4j and how to remediate).
- Thought leadership articles from CISOs to highlight the impact of this issue.
- Highlighting their "customer first" response in prospect and customer sales cycles.

While every company had to eventually respond to this issue, companies with a strong communications team were able to showcase more value to their customers.

What Does Corporate Communications Do?

From our experience, the corporate comms function typically includes external, internal, and customer comms; analyst relations; and social media. The goals of these groups are as follows:

- **External Communications:** Often referred to as public relations (PR), this function generally covers how an organization communicates with the public, including stakeholders from the media industry. This is one of the best-known and longstanding functions of corporate communications departments, as media and PR are highly visible initiatives.
- **Internal Communications:** Refers to how an organization communicates with its internal stakeholders, such as employees, managers, or leaders. Internal communications initiatives are vital because they allow organizations to streamline their operations and meet goals efficiently.

- **Customer Communications:** Refers to the ways an organization interacts with its customers or clients. Oftentimes, these communication strategies overlap with the marketing team's (for example, customer advocacy), but customer support may also handle them. In many organizations, customer communications are structured, organizationally, within the customer success and service function, but we wanted to highlight this important function.
- **Analyst Relations (AR):** A long-term activity that refers to an organization's strategy for interaction and communication with independent research and consulting firms such as Gartner, Forrester, IDC, and others.
- **Social Media Engagement:** Most enterprises reach out to the broader community via social media platforms (LinkedIn, YouTube, Twitter, etc.). Communication teams need to be adept at social listening, creating dialogue, analyzing outcomes, and developing strategies to create publicity and awareness for the organization.

Since the comms team has many different functions, core activities vary by functional need. Let's take a closer look at each.

External Communications: Public and Media Relations

PR is responsible for generating publicity and awareness to foster more sales. The goals of the PR team include media research and management, press releases and spokesperson management, and various other activities:

Media research and management

- Monitoring competitors for news and trends that affect your enterprise's awareness and position in the market.
- Identifying and cultivating relationships with top-tier journalists that cover your market.
- Creating multiple targeted lists of media contacts—business, industry, and technology press/journalists—to bring contextual messages to your media customers.

Press releases and spokesperson management
- Initiating and orchestrating regular spokesperson communications between enterprise thought leaders, executives, and SMEs with the media.
- Facilitating the press release process by creating them, along with media alerts, blogs, and other content that furthers your awareness in the right channels.
- Pitching media outlets on the story/news and secure coverage. This is very important. It's not about getting a press release out on the wire; it's about gaining coverage that is "earned" on the strength of the story and the relationships that exist.
- Monitoring and analyzing the results of PR campaigns.

Investor relations and executive platform management
- In public companies, PR teams also work closely with the company's investor relations (IR) function to ensure that financial communications, including earnings releases and call scripts, are communicated across stakeholder groups
- Finally, in many enterprises, PR teams also oversee speaker platforms where executives and thought leaders from the company can present the company story and points of view to increase visibility and impact. Key forums to track here include (but are not limited to):
- Analyst events (e.g., Gartner, Forrester, or IDC)
- Business events (e.g., World Economic Forum, etc.)
- Market events (RSA Security, Black Hat)
- Ecosystem/partner events (AWS re:Invent, Google Next, etc.)

What are the key KPIs for the PR team? While it can track a variety of metrics, here are some key ones to gauge the effectiveness of the PR function:
- **Media Outreach and Coverage:** Quantify the number of press releases and pitches you are sending out and track how they perform and the amount of coverage generated. Also, measure your progress in building relationships with

journalists. You can also track the viewership count for publications and websites where your coverage is featured.

- **Share of Voice:** Measure your percentage of coverage— for your brand, products, or high-profile executives— compared to competitors. Include several competitors to gauge your position within the industry, or benchmark them one at a time and drill into the corresponding media coverage to uncover key differentiators.

- **Sentiment of Coverage:** Also consider the sentiment of the coverage, i.e., the tone of the articles mentioning your brand or competitors. This metric lets you see if your brand is creating positive or negative associations.

- **Social Engagement:** How many shares and social comments the coverage you generate receive.

- **Stock Price (Public Companies):** Earning announce- ments, merger and acquisitions (M&A) announcements, crisis communications, and major news articles that posi- tively or negatively impact company valuation.

Internal Communications

In addition to being responsible for communicating the organization's message with external audiences, most communications teams will also play a role in internal messaging. This function is often done in collaboration with the human resources team. The role of this function is primarily to coordinate internal communications throughout the organization to keep employees engaged, aware, and informed. With that goal in mind, the internal communication team's tasks typically include:

- Drafting key messages and communications, including emails, presentations, and memos that announce company news and initiatives.

- Managing internal blogs, newsletters, intranet sites, or other internal publications.

- Compiling employee resources (such as information about employee benefits).

- Creating printed materials, such as employee handbooks or flyers.

Customer Communications

Customer communications teams are responsible for outbound communiqués to existing customers. They may send marketing materials and offers; share information about new products, services, and capabilities; and may also share information about renewals. For most organizations, the customer comms team sits within the customer success and support organization, but it can also be part of the corporate communications team. The goal is to define an effective strategy to build trusted relationships with customers so that mindshare can be captured and loyalty and retention improved. Effective customer communication can act as an engine to drive demand and fuel long-term growth.

Analyst Relations

AR teams are tasked with executing effective analyst relations programs and aligning them with corporate strategies and goals. A list of specific tasks is identified in the following table.

Table 4.1: Core Responsibilities for AR Professionals

Analyst Research	Analyst Interactions	Evaluations (MQs, Waves, etc.)	Events	Marketing Comms	Other
Identify and track relevant analysts.	Request and schedule regular, periodic briefings.	Project manage the eval process, including customer references and fact-checking.	Help plan and drive attendance to vendor-hosted events.	Partner with PR and marketing to leverage analyst relations for key activities.	Manage and negotiate annual research firm subscriptions and seats.
Monitor analyst activities (e.g., blogs, articles, social, research).	Plan and help execute presentations and demos—partnering with portfolio marketing, execs, and SMEs.	Harmonize, edit, and submit written responses—working with portfolio marketing, product management, and finance.	Work with the events team to manage event and travel logistics.	Coordinate review/approval cycles with analysts' citations departments.	Manage and negotiate report licensing.
Read and communicate key points from analyst activities.	Take notes, track action items, and coordinate follow-ups.	Plan and execute the presentations, demos, and references.	Coordinate attendance at analyst-hosted events and summarize and distribute post-event notes.	Identify what content to license and help promote licensed reports.	Coordinate delivery of entitlements (reports, webinars, etc.).
Monitor analyst research agendas to influence upcoming work.	Create and distribute quarterly comms to analysts (e.g., newsletters, key announcements, etc.).	Help explain and promote the evaluation placement internally (e.g., for sales and externally).	Ensure interactions with key analysts take place and provide prep materials like speaking points, analyst backgrounds, etc.	Work with PR/marketing to drive awareness of research inclusions.	Ensure compliance with subscription/licensing teams.

Source: Adapted from ARInsights.[2]

Pro Tip
A rule of thumb is that one analyst relations professional can effectively manage about twelve Tier 1 industry analysts at a time. Of course, there is often a long tail of Tier 1 and Tier 2 analysts that are engaged less frequently than others.

How do you measure the success of your AR program?

Although many organizations think that AR's sole job is positioning a company as a "Leader" in a Gartner Magic Quadrant (MQ), Forrester Wave, or IDC MarketScape, there are other factors to consider. Their responsibilities may include analyst reports, interactions with analysts, third-party mentions, and feedback from analysts. One should adopt a multifaceted approach to measuring the success of an AR program. The goal is to increase positive mindshare among analysts so your brand is amplified and products or services recommended to external clients. The following are a few thoughts on KPIs for AR programs.

- **Analytics Reports (MQ/Wave/MarketScape, etc.):** Analyst product bakeoff (comparative) reports are often considered the "ideal" outcome of analyst relations programs. And these reports are worth their weight in gold—especially if your company ranks well in them. However, they are generally written for a select category of products/services and have many requirements for a company placement. They are also usually the outcome of many years of thoughtful analyst relationship strategy—so hinging the entire success of your AR program on these reports alone is not advisable. Consider other KPIs to measure the success and effectiveness of your AR program.
- **Direct Analyst Interactions:** Nothing can take the place of direct analyst interactions. You need to communicate with the key analysts who cover your space to understand the market and competitive trends and keep your point of view and the innovations of your product/service on their radars.

Schedule regular inquiries, briefings, and interactions to stay on their radar screens.

- **Analyst Coverage:** Track reports (bakeoffs, market research/trend reports, vendor round-up reports) that mention your company. Also, note the sentiment of the mentions. Are they positively biased to your company's strengths?
- **Analyst Feedback:** Leverage analyst feedback in your product/service innovation lifecycle. Analyst interactions are a two-way street. Showcase your product roadmap to analysts. Get their feedback. And track how much of this feedback makes it back into your product roadmap.

Don't be the smartest person in the AR room
Many product managers and product marketers mistakenly try to convince analysts that they are the "smartest person in the room." When engaging with analysts, make sure you understand their worldview and align your portfolio and point of view to their mental map. We once had a colleague who called this the "floating balloons" technique. For each analyst, he would mention key topics that were important to the company and would create a heatmap of which topics were important to that particular analyst. We had a spreadsheet with a dozen analysts and clearly understood which topics we should discuss with each analyst. In the end, it is your job to build a genuine relationship, understand the analyst's point of view, and align your offerings to their mental map. If you create an adversarial relationship, you may be in the doghouse for years to come. AR is a long-term game.

Social Media

Social media is becoming increasingly more important and strategic for B2B software companies. This begs the question, what does the social media team do? Core activities include:

- **Identifying Social Media Platforms**: Know your ideal customer profile (ICP) and the demographics common among your target audience to figure out which platforms they use. What works for B2B enterprises? The next figure identifies the most common social media platforms used by content marketing teams.[3] The top five channels that produced the best results were LinkedIn, Facebook, Instagram, YouTube, and Twitter.[4]

Figure 4.1: Organic (Non-Paid) Social Media Platforms Used by Content Marketers

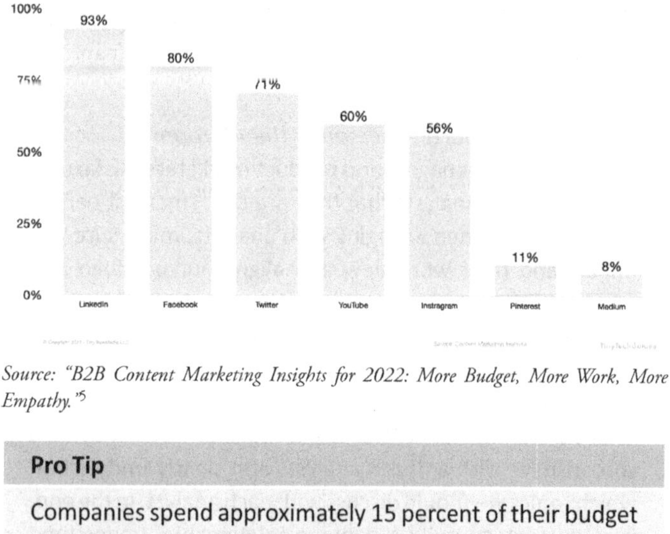

Source: "B2B Content Marketing Insights for 2022: More Budget, More Work, More Empathy."[5]

Pro Tip
Companies spend approximately 15 percent of their budget on social media. For B2B companies, LinkedIn is often a particularly valuable resource for lead generation since it's such a business-oriented platform.[6]

- **Sharing Useful Content**: B2B social marketing is all about useful content. The more informational the content, the better. Since social media content is usually a top-of-the-funnel engagement phase (think more awareness), use minimal salesy materials at this stage of the interaction. *Do* use infographics and videos to educate users about your business, products, and industry. You can also share blog posts from your site if you have a blog. If you have social proof in the form of customer testimonials, social media is a great platform to disseminate this content. As users learn more about you and what you do, they'll become more open to buying from you.

> **Pro Tip**
>
> Many companies we have worked for have set up social media amplification platforms (e.g., Hootsuite, Buffer, etc.) to allow internal employees to easily share approved content across a variety of channels. This helps amplify the company's message.

- **Interacting, Interacting, Interacting**: Social media is an interactive medium. If there's one thing you should never forget to do, it's to interact with your audience. By "interact," we don't mean talk *at them*, we mean talk *with them*. It's called social media—your communication should be bi-directional. When people tag you or ask you questions, be sure to respond.
- **Measuring, Optimizing, and Repeating**: Companies need to put in a framework to measure the impact of their social media strategy. These need to move beyond the simple engagement metrics (i.e., likes, shares, and comments), as these often fail to correlate to business value. Companies need to tie social media metrics to business outcomes. Ultimately, you are trying to convert your prospective buyers into paying customers. To measure the success of social media programs, people can look at reach (followers and growth rates, impressions, and traffic to the website). There are engagement metrics (likes, shares, comments, and clicks) and conversion metrics (click-through rates, cost per click, and conversion rates). Monitor these metrics carefully and continually optimize the social media program based on customer behavior.

Who Makes a Good Corporate Communications Professional?

As seen above, corporate communications strategies have a variety of functions. Most departments enlist professionals who specialize in each function of communications to collaborate efficiently and engage target audiences appropriately.

However, there are a few core skills that are common across all members of a comms team:

- A love of the written word and a gift for communicating complex issues clearly and credibly with a wide variety of audiences.
- Storytelling abilities combined with excellent persuasive skills. Messaging conveyed through personal stories (e.g., a customer's problem solved or an internal challenge addressed) always resonates better, so the comms teams should try to personalize messages to make them memorable.
- Tenacity. When you're pitching to the media, you may hear "no" a thousand times before hearing your first "yes." You need tough skin to march on—even in the face of rejection.
- The ability to work well with internal executives and stakeholders to define the company messaging.

KPIs for Corporate Communications

There are a myriad of metrics and KPIs that are used by organizations to measure the impact of corporate communications. These often include:

- PR metrics
  - Share of voice
  - Earned media coverage
  - Number of bylines and mentions in articles
  - Number of impressions of articles
  - Quality of media coverage (Tier 1, business press, etc., versus Tier 2 press, technology, etc.)
  - Pipeline driven by PR activities (press releases, articles, etc.)

- AR metrics
  - AR report mentions
  - AR report placements
  - Sales opportunities with analyst support (actively referred/influenced or passive via reports, etc.)
  - Analysts' sentiment and perception (including before-and-after surveys given directly to individual analysts)

- Social media metrics
  - Number of social media posts per week/month
  - Social media engagement
  - Quality of social media engagement (ideal customer profile versus rest, etc.)

- Other
  - Website reviews

Practical Advice and Next Steps

- **Expectation Setting**: Every CEO wants their company to be recognized as a trusted brand and thought leader, including analyst accolades like a Leader's Quadrant placement in Gartner MQ or Forrester Wave. Many companies don't elegantly fit into an analyst category, and fewer still have all the right capabilities to win in a category. Communication teams have the tough job of tempering the expectations of the executive team while continuing to engage with analysts to drive awareness for their category and product suite.
- **Aligning PR and Media Outreach to Interesting Topics**: The press follows and writes articles about topics that are relevant to current conversations. Find ways to insert yourself into those discussions. If it's Super Bowl season, find ways to talk about how you support football or any other sport. If it's tax season, talk dollars and cents.
- **Identifying Differentiated Talking Points**: Don't follow the herd. Take a provocative point of view (POV) and/or provide something of interest. Anything data-related works

best here. If you can back up your POV with facts and statistics, the media will always be interested in the story.

Summary

In this chapter, we learned:

- The corporate comms team has a wide range of responsibilities, including AR, PR, internal comms, customer comms, and social media.
- AR is a long-term relationship. Consider the "floating balloons" technique and create a heatmap of topics that resonate with every analyst.
- As Gen Z and millennials gain increased buying power, social media is increasingly important for organizations. Consider the right channel for the right goal (i.e., LinkedIn for demand gen).

Chapter 4 References

[1] "2022 Edelman Trust Barometer." Edelman. Accessed April 23, 2023. https://www.edelman.com/trust/2022-trust-barometer.

[2] Zimmerman, Andy. "The Analyst Relations Job Description." ARInsights. Accessed January 2, 2023. https://www.arinsights.com/analyst-relations-best-practices/the-analyst-relations-job-description/.

[3] Stahl, Stephanie. "B2B Content Marketing Insights for 2022: More Budget, More Work, More Empathy." Content Marketing Institute. October 13, 2021. https://contentmarketinginstitute.com/articles/b2b-power-content-marketing-research/.

[4] Stahl. "B2B Content Marketing Insights for 2022."

[5] Stahl. "B2B Content Marketing Insights for 2022."

[6] Moorman, Christine. "The CMO Survey: Marketing in a Post COVID Era." The CMO Survey. September, 2022. https://cmosurvey.org/results/september-2022/.

CHAPTER 5

Content, Thought Leadership, Influencers, and Communities

What Is Content Marketing ?

We've all gone to the movies—only to be disappointed. Despite all of the hype surrounding different productions, the movie just didn't do it for us. If you're curious, there's quite an impressive list of box office bombs on Wikipedia. Some movies that bombed at the box office became classics. The Christmas staple *It's a Wonderful Life* (1946) bombed at the box office but came to be one of the most iconic movies of all time. *The Shawshank Redemption* (1994), *The Big Lebowski* (1998), and *Hook* (1991), with the comedic legend Robin Williams and Oscar-winner Dustin Hoffman, also fall into the from-bomb-to-beloved category.[1] Despite budgets over $130 million for some of these films, they flopped.

That begs the question, "What causes one piece of content (in this case, a movie) to succeed while others fail?" We're sure the studios did their homework and followed a proven process to create the movie. But this is the challenge for modern marketing organizations: Despite our best intentions, some content succeeds and some falls flat. For content marketers in the B2B world, it is important to be innovative, iterative, and focused on performance.

What exactly is content marketing? It includes the process of planning, creating, distributing, sharing, and publishing content and measuring its performance via various digital and offline channels, such as social media, blogs, websites, podcasts, apps, press releases, print publications, media interviews, and more. The key is to deliver the right content, at the right time, to the prospective buyer or customer—wherever they are on their journey.

But there are also a lot of nuances to consider. Shawn Rogers, an analytics strategy thought leader, industry influencer, and marketing executive, stated in an interview with David:

> As the buyer's journey has shifted, interacting with prospects during their journey has become more difficult and often takes place outside of traditional direct channels. Content marketing utilizes various types of content to engage these prospects. Thought leadership, educational, customer-driven, and product content are all parts of this strategy.

Why Is Content Marketing Important?

In B2B marketing, a buying committee must be convinced that our products and services are the best choices to overcome the problems it's facing. Remember the difference between B2C and B2B marketing? In B2B marketing, we need to capture leads and help move them through a sales funnel/buyer's journey. The way to achieve this is through compelling, engaging, and informative content. But what defines a good piece of content? According to Rogers:

> Prospects generally consume five to seven pieces of content (or more) during their journey toward engaging with vendors, and many of these interactions take place at locations other than a vendor's website. So, it's critical for companies to promote content into the marketplace to engage prospects starting with the research phase of their journey. While obtaining a sales

lead is the ultimate goal of a content marketing strategy, first and foremost, content needs to bolster brand recognition and reputation of the brand while being educational, influential, and effective for thought leadership. The key is to avoid over-rotating on the seller's brand and product while adding value.

What Makes Content Good?

Now, the Internet is full of uninteresting, dull, and unoriginal content. Most of the content we read is a rehash of some other article—now likely written by artificial intelligence (AI). Having a background in science, we often check the references of articles we read only to find they are nonexistent. (Really, it's important to make sure you gather your content from actual, trusted sources). To define "good" content, we'll take a pragmatic approach.

Good content is:

- **Informative**: While good content is designed to teach, educate, and inform prospects about the products and services you offer, it should first and foremost tell readers something they don't know. It needs to grab their attention with an original thought or message.

- **Consumable and Compelling**: Good content is snackable (short and to the point), digestible, and targeted toward your target audience (market segment and persona), but it should also grab readers with words, images, or stories that are different and interesting.

- **Converts**: Effective content will trigger your prospect to take the next step in the buyer's journey by showcasing how your products and services solve challenges through real-world examples. Experience has shown that content that focuses on alleviating buyers' challenges performs better than content that touts gains.

- **Builds Trust**: Good content builds relationships between your customers and your business that result in increased loyalty and create a sense of community around your brand.

- **The Right Format**: Good content takes on a variety of formats to increase relevancy to the personas you are targeting.

- **The Right Place**: High-performing content is distributed to the right digital channels for your target personas. It needs to meet buyers on their channel of preference, at the right time, and with the right message.
- **Findable**: You won't always know exactly where to find your prospective customers. You should make your content "findable" by ensuring strong SEO elements are applied.

When Rogers was asked about what makes content good, he said:

> The short answer is value-based content first, brand and product a distant second. Tech buyers have changed, and boomers are no longer making most of the purchasing decisions. New digital-driven buyers want easy access to the information they seek when making decisions. They're not interested in hearing about your product at every interaction; they want to do business with market leaders and partners who bring a deep understanding of the industry, are validated by third-party influencers and experts, and go beyond just selling to them.

One other consideration for creating good content is deciding how it gets regionalized. In many B2B organizations, there is a hub-and-spoke model for regional marketing teams scattered throughout the world. There is often a centralized team that creates content and works with the demand gen teams to create "programs in a box." The content created by this centralized team is then picked up by the regional teams for appropriate localization and translation. You have to make sure your content is not specific to any one geographic region, and also consider the language used with regard to any translations that may occur. For example, you may want to avoid using metaphors (e.g., it all went pear-shaped) or specific events (e.g., U.S.—only holidays like Thanksgiving and the 4th of July) that may not be relevant in other markets.

We had the opportunity to pose the "great content" question to Naomi Miller, a senior brand and corporate communications leader:

> The primary attribute of "great content" is it teaches you something you didn't know and that the vendor providing it has a unique perspective or set of data to validate its point of view (POV). In the beginning stages of the sales process, customers don't want to be sold to; they want to learn something new and gain insights in their area of interest.

Next, ensure that you have a feedback loop from the regional teams to the centralized teams. There may be different themes, topics, and concepts that resonate in some parts of the world that the centralized team may not be aware of.

Now that we understand a few guiding principles for creating good content, what types do B2B organizations create?

The Content B2B Organizations Create

Such content is varied and prolific. This is not an exhaustive list, but in our experience, we have created:

- Whitepapers
- Data sheets
- Solution briefs
- Website copy
- Digital ad copy
- Total cost of ownership (TCO) calculators
- Maturity calculators (of an organizational discipline, function, or practice)
- Product tours
- Surveys
- Demos
- Newspaper articles
- Press releases
- Frequently asked questions (FAQs)
- Explainer videos
- Sizzle videos

- Third-party research
- Webinars
- Event presentations (keynotes and breakouts)
- Podcasts
- Radio shows
- TV appearances
- Infographics
- Animated videos
- Customer story videos
- Case studies
- Technical explainer videos
- Technical papers
- Surveys
- Books

One firm we worked for was a SaaS company that monitored the performance and security of applications running in cloud environments. Many SaaS companies have a unique advantage in their sales model—they have access to how their customers are using their product (also known as telemetry data). This can provide unique insights about customer usage and behavior, which is much sought after in any market.

With this goal in mind, the product marketing team worked with our customer success team to aggregate and anonymize our SaaS data. After analyzing it, we got a treasure trove of cloud usage insights. Few other companies had this data—at scale and in real-life usage. We pulled together tens of charts and insights into a unique "State of the Cloud" report, which became an excellent thought leadership piece as well a door opener for the company. Finally, the content team took this asset a step further. It started to generate year-over-year trends from the data, creating wonderful blogs and other assets that would amplify the core content even more. As you can see, a few good minds working on the data concept—customer success, product marketing, and content marketing —were able to create a prolific set of differentiated content for the company.

AI-Generated Content

ChatGPT is an artificial intelligence program that was created by OpenAI, which states on its blog: "We've trained a model called ChatGPT which interacts conversationally. The dialogue format makes it possible for ChatGPT to answer follow-up questions, admit its mistakes, challenge incorrect premises, and reject inappropriate requests."

This may be one of the most transformative technologies out there, and its impact on marketing may forever change the landscape. Microsoft has invested more than US$1 billion in OpenAI and recently signed a multiyear investment with OpenAI worth billions. ChatGPT will be embedded in Microsoft's Bing search engine and it's expected to embed it in many other products. In addition to ChatGPT, which can automatically create (mostly) coherent text, OpenAI also has software called DALL-E 2 which can generate images.

ChatGPT and other generative AI technologies will allow marketing organizations to quickly create short-form and medium-form content without the aid of a human. It is likely that PR teams will no longer have to write press releases— ChatGPT will do it. No longer will ad specialists need to write ad copy—AI will do it for you. The focus of marketing teams will shift towards ensuring the content is unique, conveying the message creatively, and distributing content to the right channels. Many content marketers will be editing generative AI content, rather than creating it from scratch.

However, ChatGPT will struggle to create longer-form, thought leadership-type content. It can create faux examples, but it will not be original content since it can only regurgitate what it has been trained on. Marketing teams also will need to be careful about any copyright infringements, biases, racism, sexism, plagiarism, and accuracy. As of the writing of this book, the buzz and hype surrounding ChatGPT is at an all-time high and we are excited to see how things evolve.

When ChatGPT was asked how it will impact marketing, this is what it said:

As an AI language model, ChatGPT can have a significant impact on B2B marketing. Here are a few ways:

1. **Personalized Conversational Marketing:** ChatGPT can help B2B companies engage in personalized conversations with potential customers. By using natural language processing, ChatGPT can understand the needs and preferences of individual customers and provide them with customized recommendations.

2. **Content Creation:** B2B companies can leverage ChatGPT's capabilities to generate content ideas and create compelling content for target audiences. ChatGPT can analyze data from multiple sources, including social media, search engines, and industry trends, to generate unique and relevant content ideas.

3. **Lead Generation:** ChatGPT can assist B2B companies in lead generation by engaging potential customers in real-time conversations. By providing valuable information and guidance, ChatGPT can help companies establish a relationship with potential customers and convert them into leads.

4. **Customer Service:** B2B companies can use ChatGPT to provide customer service to clients. It can quickly and accurately respond to customer inquiries, resolve issues, and provide solutions, improving customer satisfaction and loyalty.

5. **Predictive Analytics:** B2B companies can use ChatGPT to analyze customer data and gain insights into customer behavior and preferences. By using predictive analytics, companies can optimize marketing strategies and improve ROI.

In summary, ChatGPT's capabilities can help B2B companies improve marketing efforts, increase customer engagement, and ultimately drive revenue growth.

Pro Tip

In our experience, content marketing teams—which include not only strategists but also writers and designers—are chronically under-resourced. Rather than worrying about how generative AI will adversely impact you, think about how you can proactively embrace what it's good at and apply your bandwidth to higher-value, more strategic activities.

How to Build an Effective Content Marketing Strategy

Now that we understand what good content looks like, let's look at how you can take the steps to create a content marketing strategy. Here are seven steps to follow:

1. **Identify Your Segment and Audience**: Use persona and messaging guides to understand your target audience and market segment.
2. **Define Your Objectives**: Before you begin a content marketing strategy, define your business objectives and purpose.
3. **Understand What You Have**: Many organizations have no idea about the content they have, how old it is, or its performance metrics (suddenly remember that landing page that was uploaded three years ago?). Conduct a content audit to understand what exists, how old it is, and its performance across all media—your website, YouTube, sales enablement, etc.
4. **Determine Content Type and Derivative Content Type**: Since different people react and consume content in different ways, your content should take a variety of forms. For example, if you conduct a webinar, then follow up with a short social video, a blog, and a written piece to supplement the original.

5. **Create a Distribution Strategy**: Work with your cross-functional teams to understand and define how your content will be activated in the market.

6. **Create a Distribution Plan**: Create a content calendar to share and align cross-functional teams on what content will be created, when it will go live, and how it will be distributed.

7. **Measure, Analyze, and Optimize**: Create a measurement system to track content performance across multiple channels and use frequent test and learn cycles to optimize outcomes.

Pro Tip

Many organizations we have worked with have a decent understanding of gated content (content behind a registration form). However, a holistic view remains elusive to many organizations. Spend time developing a complete view of all content—across all of your web properties, digital channels, and all stages of the buyer's journey.

The next figure is a content map template that we have seen used in many organizations.

Figure 5.1: Content Map Template

TinyTechGuides - Content Map Template for <Persona>

Thought Leadership & Awareness	Consideration	Closing	Adoption
Blogs, Articles & Podcasts	E-Books, White Papers & Reports	E-Books, White Papers & Reports	Webinars, Videos & How-Tos
• TBD 1 • TBD 2 • TBD 3	• TBD 1 • TBD 2 • TBD 3	• TBD 1 • TBD 2 • TBD 3	• TBD 1 • TBD 2 • TBD 3
Videos & Infographics	Webinars & Videos	Webinars & Videos	Customer Stories
• TBD 1 • TBD 2 • TBD 3	• TBD 1 • TBD 2 • TBD 3	• TBD 1 • TBD 2 • TBD 3	• TBD 1 • TBD 2 • TBD 3
Reports, Briefs & Pages	Customer Stories	Reports, Briefs & Pages	Reports, Briefs & Pages
• TBD 1 • TBD 2 • TBD 3	• TBD 1 • TBD 2 • TBD 3	• TBD 1 • TBD 2 • TBD 3	• TBD 1 • TBD 2 • TBD 3

© Copyright 2023 - TinyTechMedia LLC

How Does Content Marketing Work?

Businesses can use content marketing to attract leads, make a case for their solutions to potential buyers, and close sales. To use it effectively, the right content needs to be delivered at each stage of the customer's journey and sales cycle —from awareness through consideration to purchase.

Let's look at how this process really works. The next figure illustrates how companies use content marketing at each stage of the sales cycle to engage and sell to prospects.

Figure 5.2: Content Marketing Process

Many organizations often view this in terms of a funnel that we will describe in Chapter 6.

Awareness Content

At the awareness or top-of-funnel (TOFU) stage of the sales process, content should focus on the most important concerns of your audience. Writing about their pain points, challenges, and questions provides the best chance of engaging with them. Content at the awareness stage should be un-gated and educational how-to advice. Save the selling for the consideration and closing phases.

Consideration Content

The consideration stage or middle-of-the-funnel (MOFU) stage should offer helpful hybrid content that is both informative and market-driven. It should educate the reader about what features or functions to look for in a solution and show how various features address their needs. Naturally, content should lean toward what your business offers.

Closing Content

When a prospect is close to buying, content marketing plays an important role. At the bottom-of-the-funnel stage (BOFU), focus on selling the specific virtues of your product or solution—continue to drive home why you're the best choice based on their particular needs, as opposed to just reiterating how great your services or products are. Your central message here should be your expertise, knowledge, and the differentiating benefits of your product or service.

Adoption Content

After the sale, many organizations have customer success teams who create content to facilitate the adoption and usage of the product or service. These generally address things like onboarding and how-to content that teaches users how to get the most out of the product or service. This type of content is often sent via email, included in community content, or built directly into the software application (with features like in-product tutorials). After all, if customers don't have a pleasant onboarding experience and fail to use the product, they will not be customers for very long. Forget about word-of-mouth sales.

Advocacy or Customer Content

Don't forget to close the loop and develop a strategy for systematically following up with successful customers in order to market their stories. Include case studies about how customers found you and how their implementations went. Most of all, attempt to get customers to describe the quantitative outcomes achieved using your solution. This social proof is **gold** when it comes to creating content that resonates with prospective customers across the buyer's journey. The following table summarizes the different content types.

Table 5.1: Content Types by Stage

	Awareness	Consideration	Closing	Adoption
Content Aim & Type	TOFU awareness engagement	MOFU evaluation engagement	BOFU purchase engagement	Retention / advocacy engagement
B2B Examples	• Thought leadership • Infographics • 10X content • Educational webinars • Explainer videos	• Case studies • Data Sheets • Independent reviews • Webinars • Demos • Technical videos	• ROI calculators • Business case • Video use-case examples	• Career Development • Newsletters • Product/solution how-to/tips/tricks videos • Discussion boards/knowledge bases
Distribution	• SEO • Social media • Digital ads	• Email welcome • Email nurture • Newsletters • Web personalization • Live chat	• Email from sales (automated) • Webinars	• Email Newsletters • Web personalization

Source: Adapted from "TOFU vs MOFU vs BOFU Content."[2]

Types of Content

Thought Leadership Content

A component of both brand (see Chapter 3) and demand generation (see Chapter 7), thought leadership content is designed to provide education and expertise. Generally, it does not talk about a company's specific products or services. Rather, it is designed to let prospective buyers know that a company, and often selected employees within a company, have expertise in a certain domain. Thought leadership content builds trust and mindshare among prospective buyers. Thought leaders are often experts in their field and act as trusted advisors.

Thought leadership stems from a person's own mind that pioneers intellectual property, spawning concepts that inspire and move others into action. They tend to have a finger on the pulse of enterprise, creating a brand that promises to foster not just communal trust but universal subscription.[3]

Shawn Rogers said:

> The best thought leaders have deep industry knowledge, maintain vendor neutrality, and deliver significant audience reach and engagement. Successful thought leaders take a position on important industry topics and share that point of view widely. Thought leaders who partner with vendors deliver unique engagement channels that are not often found within the vendor's business ecosystem.

Influencer Content

In contrast with thought leadership content, influencer marketing tends to be biased toward brand building and then demand generation. We're not saying that you cannot generate leads from influencers; rather, in our experience, we tend to see it as an awareness play. Influencer content is material that is generated by third parties who have an established following in your market on a certain channel. For B2B, these channels are typically LinkedIn, YouTube, and Twitter, though we expect to see a shift to shorter-form content as millennials increase their influence in organizations. Influencers can be paid or not paid by an organization.

Rogers explained:

> Influencers can extend a brand's message deeper into the market and catch the attention of buyers early on in the buyer's journey. There are many vehicles to choose from, including guest blog posts, expert articles/whitepapers, social augmentation, speaking at vendor events, and so forth. Influencers play the role of third-party validation and can help build a brand's reputation in the market.

Community Content

This is generated by software users and can be quite powerful for an organization. Unfortunately, for most of the companies we have worked for, community content is generally underutilized. What better source to communicate the benefits and value of your products and services than the actual users of your software? Community content, if organized correctly, can also act as a knowledge base that can reduce the number of support personnel needed. Think about this—if there's a question on how to use your software, who better to answer it than a peer, as opposed to having to open a support ticket?

Get a Handle On Your Content

Most organizations have more content than they realize and usually don't have a good handle on what exists. There are tools like digital asset management (DAM) systems that can help with the content creation process and act as a centralized repository for your organization's output. Unfortunately, we have yet to work with an organization that has a DAM system. A Forrester survey found that 50 percent of the organizations surveyed have been using a DAM for less than two years.[4]

Who Makes the Best B2B Content Marketers?

Shawn Rogers has hired many content marketers. He looks for the following qualities:

Imagination and a fierce focus on valuable content. Most content marketers are often on opposite sides of traditional marketing strategies. Applying a 'measure-everything attitude' to the content and programs is the key to disrupting older, more traditional strategies. Advertising models continue to deliver lower ROI than the more sophisticated content marketing programs.

Best KPIs for B2B Content Marketing

Now that you have a perspective on what good content is and how to build an effective content marketing strategy, let's take a look at how to measure success. Below are some of the most common metrics and KPIs used in marketing organizations:

1. **Website Traffic:** Getting more clients and prospects to visit your company website is a crucial goal for content marketers. By using a tool like Google Analytics, you can measure traffic, the number of new visitors, and how your website and its content were discovered. This will help identify and resolve issues regarding site traffic.

2. **Marketing-Qualified Leads (MQLs)**: Leads that have consumed your content and taken some action that suggests an interest in your product/service. Analyzing which MQLs match your company's typical client profile helps identify higher-quality leads and improve the chances of conversion.

3. **Conversion Per Activity:** This KPI measures the number of conversions per activity, such as clicking on a call-to-action (CTA), website visits, etc. It allows you to understand the impact of your landing and confirmation pages in guiding prospects to your website.

4. **Cost Per Lead (CPLs):** A KPI that evaluates the cost of obtaining each lead across different marketing channels. This provides insight into how effective and costly your content marketing campaign is per potential customer.

5. **Engagement:** A simple and clever way to evaluate the effectiveness of content in attracting clients is to simply quantify clicks. These can indicate brand awareness and engagement, which further conveys the effectiveness of your marketing campaigns.

6. **Revenue Contributed:** Finally, evaluate how well your content marketing efforts are paying off. Measure individual marketing campaign ROIs to get the bigger picture of how content marketing performance is contributing to revenue.

Day-to-Day Activities of the Content Marketing Leader

What does the content marketing leader do? The content marketing manager needs to engage with stakeholders from across the organization and has a wide range of responsibilities:

- Gain customer understanding to determine who to target and identify pain points and topics to write content about. Understand the challenges faced by each buyer persona and use them to create targeted content campaigns addressing and solving challenges.
- Collaborate closely with the marketing team to both identify and leverage content across paid and owned marketing channels that will drive awareness and growth. Work closely with product, customer success, and marketing partners to identify relevant topics, customer stories, and timely content themes.
- Develop content strategy (e.g., pillar strategy) and core content ownership areas.
- Lead all content marketing initiatives, including creating and managing the content calendar and driving desired brand perception, traffic, and leads from content marketing.
- Plan, develop, and implement insight-driven, high-value thought leadership content strategy, including thought leadership blogs, whitepapers, e-books, customer case studies, video scripts, and data sheets.
- Own SEO and email marketing initiatives.
- Measure and analyze content-related metrics on a regular basis and factor results into future content recommendations and developments.
- Help create a content calendar and manage the scheduling and release of a steady stream of engaging top-, mid-, and bottom-funnel content.
- Research, outline, and write persona-targeted materials that fuel marketing campaigns, including e-books, webinars, web pages, blog posts, videos, and more.

Practical Advice and Next Steps

- Conduct an audit of your existing content and determine if you should update it, keep it as is, or delete it.
- Form a cross-functional team to understand what content is needed, how it will be used, and by whom.
- Create a content calendar, measurement system, and process to keep your content continuously up-to-date and fresh.

Summary

- We examined the attributes of good content—which is designed to educate and inform, is snackable and relevant, and delivered to the right audience on the right channel at the right time.
- We discussed how to build an effective content strategy and create a content map.
- We looked at the day-to-day activities of the content marketing leader.

Chapter 5 References

[1] Hayes, Allie. "21 Movies That Did 'Meh' at the Box Office, but People Love Them Anyway." BuzzFeed. November 17, 2022. https://www.buzzfeed.com/alliehayes/movies-that-bombed-but-we-love-them-reddit.

[2] Chaffey, Dave. "TOFU vs MOFU vs BOFU Content." Dr Dave Chaffey: Digital Insights. July 8, 2020. https://www.davechaffey.com/digital-marketing-glossary/tofu-vs-mofu-vs-bofu-content/.

[3] Michail, Jon. "What Is Thought Leadership and How Does It Benefit Your Business?" *Forbes*. April 4, 2022. https://www.forbes.com/sites/forbescoachescouncil/2022/04/04/what-is-thought-leadership-and-how-does-it-benefit-your-business/.

[4] Barber, Nick. "Get Your DAM House in Order: Latest Forrester WaveTM Highlights Top DAM Vendors." Forrester. February 16, 2022. https://www.forrester.com/blogs/get-your-dam-house-in-order-forrester-wave-highlights-top-dam-vendors/.

CHAPTER 6

Demand Generation

What Is Demand Gen?

In practical terms, demand generation (DG) is an overarching range of marketing activities that create buyer interest and long-term engagement, ultimately delivering superior MQLs. Demand gen activities include a series of interactions and touchpoints designed to raise awareness of customer challenges, position your brand as a trusted advisor, generate leads, sell your solution, and foster genuine brand loyalty.

Demand generation activities may include online (digital) as well as offline channels. Digital marketing includes activities like paid media, email marketing, social media marketing, and so forth. Offline channels include trade shows, networking receptions, direct mailings, and other in-person activities. From a budget perspective, 56 percent of marketing budgets are typically allocated to digital, while 44 percent are allocated to offline channels.[1] We suspect that increasing shares of budgets will continue to shift towards digital channels as marketing continues to evolve.

Demand generation is a data-driven marketing strategy focused on driving awareness and interest in an organization's products and services, with the ultimate goal of developing long-term customer engagement. Demand generation includes lead capture, lead nurturing, and pipeline acceleration.[2]

Why Is Demand Gen Important?

If customers aren't aware of it, then having a solution to their problems really isn't much of a solution. Being aware of a brand is critically important. Even very large, well-known brands have to make customers aware of their specific product and solution offerings—think AWS, a part of the world-renowned Amazon brand.

Do you recall the 812 CRM vendors in Figure 3.3? This is the kind of situation where demand generation campaigns shine—they create the required **product awareness** with the right audiences. Then, they provide targeted techniques (e.g., programs or campaigns) that identify and cultivate these potential customers, resulting in the generation of high-quality leads with an increased likelihood of conversion to the opportunities pipeline. In our experience, demand gen teams are increasingly accountable for the volume of sales opportunities and the size of the sales pipeline, not just "leads."

GTM Campaigns

Before the DG team starts executing demand gen activities, it's critical for the product, marketing, sales, and customer success teams to align on how the company targets, markets, and sells its solutions. GTM campaigns (sometimes also referred to as "plays") are the core foundation of this alignment.

Every B2B company wants to grow. It builds a product or service to solve a customer problem, then hires GTM teams to position, articulate, and differentiate the product's capabilities, including sellers to close deals and customer success to ensure usage and adoption. But this process seldom works because there is often a weak connection between the GTM strategy and actual execution.

The answer to bridging the gap is GTM campaigns.

> GTM campaigns are the golden thread that connects strategy and execution. They ensure alignment across the product, sales, marketing, and customer success teams into a cohesive, data-driven system. Pragmatically, an organization will typically have around five active GTM campaigns or plays at any given time.

Planning and documenting your GTM campaigns ensure alignment across the entire organization. Marketing teams can take an integrated approach to execute a repeatable set of programs and tactics that provide the sales teams with the best possible leads and opportunities. This alignment also ensures that sales teams are trained, ready, and capable of prospecting and nurturing the leads with the best knowledge and process available to close deals. Lastly, the GTM operations team can measure activities and results across all of the sales plays, providing valuable data-driven feedback to the marketing and sales teams so they can continually optimize and refine their plays.

It should be noted that some companies also refer to these campaigns as "marketing campaigns" or "sales plays." We think these activities have to align well across the product, marketing, sales, and customer success functions and hence prefer to call these GTM campaigns. As the partner ecosystems continue to gain importance, it is also critical to include and align your GTM activities with your partners.

Typical elements of a GTM campaign

How do you plan a GTM campaign? First, start with the basics. Before planning, you need to understand the two foundational elements of your selling proposition—your prospective buyer and the value proposition (why should prospective buyers select your solution over others) of your solution.

- **Buyer Insights**: Know your buyer, ideal customer profile (ICP), and their problems. What is the impact of the problem? What are the alternative solutions buyers would consider? Who is the competition? Where would you find the buyer? Know and document these personas and challenges. These buyers should be based on the personas discussed in Chapter 2.

- **Campaign Theme and Message**: Working with marketing, sales, and other stakeholders, develop the value proposition message and content to target your market and buyer personas. The ideal message is differentiated and addresses the business concerns and technical needs of your buyer personas. Create an easy-to-digest message, using language that your buyer would use. Again, these should be documented in the messaging guide discussed in Chapter 2.

Once the buyer and the campaign theme/message have been defined, you can plan the core programs that will define your GTM integrated campaign. Most campaigns have three programs, with many tactics within them. The major programs include:

- **Awareness Programs:** Designed to build interest, engagement, and preference by targeting key buyers and influencers within a market. They highlight the buyers' awareness of a need or show how a solution can address the problem in a compelling and differentiated way. Reputation programs leverage tactics such as PR /media, digital advertising, trade shows, peer networking events, and social media and often use top-of-funnel content to create demand in relevant markets. Awareness programs often use content from brand activities (see Chapter 3) as well as thought leadership and influencer content (see Chapter 5).

- **Demand Programs:** These create and nurture demand based on the campaign theme. They identify viable prospects and engage them in buying cycles across the buyer's journey (discussed below) through several tactics. If prospects are not yet ready to enter a buying cycle, or are stalled at a certain stage, marketing can build, maintain, or rekindle relationships. This is done via lead nurturing strategies until the buyers are ready to move forward.
- **Sales Enablement Programs:** Help sales and/or partner organizations move opportunities forward, accelerate the pipeline, navigate their prospects' buying cycles, and engage with customers. Sales enablement programs include tactics that support sales throughout the buying cycle, typically after a lead has been qualified (discussed later in this chapter). They also provide training on buyer personas and how to engage with them.
- **Customer Success:** The customer success team helps clients adopt your product, solution, or service so they receive the value promised, which additionally also creates trusted relationships that the sales teams can use for expansion plays (discussed below).

Types of GTM campaigns

From our decades of experience, we have identified four major types of GTM campaigns frequently used by organizations:

- **Land Campaign**: Designed to target new buyers. In some cases, these campaigns can be used to target decision-makers in new industry verticals, lines of business, or geographies. In other cases, they can be used to package or bundle individual products as a solution for new buyers' needs.
- **Expand Campaign**: As the name indicates, designed to sell more of your wares to existing customers. Often geared towards selling the same products, services, or solutions to new buyers within an existing company. These approaches can also help expand a company's revenue with an existing client when a seller's growth strategy has evolved.

- **Competitive Campaign**: Competitive sales plays are a great example of an evolved growth strategy because they can be deployed to exploit a competitor's weakness. Some companies engage in competitive campaigns, while others shy away from them depending on their risk tolerance.
- **Ecosystem and Partner Campaign**: Generally focusing on selling your value proposition to customers who typically use your product along with other partner solutions within the ecosystems.

How to create a GTM campaign

Start with your sales teams. They are usually adept at identifying patterns of sales. Ask them what works. These patterns may also be mined using analytics from your CRM systems. Common questions to pose to the sales team include:

- What problem and solution pitches are most effective? (Take these ideas, then expand and scale them. For example, in an enterprise, sales would typically do very well selling to the chief financial officer. Create a CFO GTM plan—a set of messages, content, ads, campaigns, and offers to target these buyer personas.)
- What competition do you go up against? Who can you beat—and with what messages/content/offers? (That could be a good GTM "displace XYZ competitor/vendor" campaign.)
- What is your product set? (See what products make for good "land and expand" sales, or sales where you contract with one user or department and then gradually sell to more of the organization. Explore if it makes sense to create new campaigns for these product sets.)
- What personas do you sell to? Is there a compelling GTM campaign that you can create for them? (At another enterprise company we were at, we sold security solutions to the chief information security officer (CISO) within

organizations. These personas were very demanding about ensuring the security of their applications when moving data to the cloud; we ideated on a "Bullet Proof Security in the Cloud" GTM campaign targeted at these personas.)

How many GTM campaigns should a company consider?
GTM campaigns require time to ideate, plan, and execute. Hence, most marketing teams can only implement a few of these at a time. A rough rule of thumb is to have around five GTM motions in the market. While we have seen some companies do more (which can be done with large marketing teams), it helps to limit motions to a handful so you can focus on a few items—and execute them well.

Now that we understand that GTM campaigns help align the entire organization and the four major types of campaigns, what materials are needed to launch a campaign?

GTM campaigns: Bill of materials
Before developing a GTM campaign bill of materials (BOM), you need to understand the focus of the play. Here are five simple steps to help with planning:

1. **Identify Target Areas of Focus and Objectives**: Assuming alignment with corporate business objectives, ensure that you have a clear set of KPIs in place, and agreement on how success will be measured. Typically, this is tracked by pipeline contribution.

2. **Define Your Target Segments**: Clearly understand the target personas, geographies, and market segments your campaign is targeting.

3. **Determine Content Needs**: Understand what content is needed by marketing and sales enablement to execute and operationalize the campaign.

4. **Identify Programs and Channels**: Identify the specific program, tactics, channels, and budget that will be used to execute the campaign.

5. **Measure, Optimize, and Refine**: Make sure the right data collection, analytics, and measurement strategies are in place so you can understand the efficacy of the campaign. Quickly optimize and refine it based on the relevant metrics and KPIs.

GTM campaigns include a set of prescriptive content that help executes plays across the marketing and sales teams. Example content for sales plays include:

Foundational Strategy Documents
- **Ideal Customer Profile and Target Personas**: These are crucial. After all, you are selling a product and services to a buying group and a set of user personas. You need to understand their preferences, watering holes, and needs.
- **Persona-Based Messaging:** This involves common pains, negative consequences, positive business outcomes, required capabilities, key differentiators, and supporting proof points for the GTM plays.

Marketing Content
- **Campaigns Program Guides**: Campaigns and tactics that should be delivered with each GTM play.
- **Campaign Content**: TOFU, MOFU, and BOFU content aligned to the buyer's journey that can be provided/shared with prospects.

Sales Content
- **Email Templates**: Create email and LinkedIn InMail templates that the sales team is encouraged to tailor as appropriate.
- **Prospecting Guides:** Equip sales with the right words (including recommended discovery questions, business value-based positioning points, ways to overcome common objections, and potential services to attach).

- **Sales Guides:** Steps and tactics to execute the campaign, including suggestions for how to leverage various partner types.
- **Competitive Battle Cards:** These help differentiate and position your offering relative to key competitors in the market.
- **Top-Performing Content**: Featured BOFU assets to share with customers and prospects.
- **Target Account Lists:** Focused sales plays that will also include target account and/or contact lists.

Next, let's take a closer look at the typical demand generation process.

Understanding the Typical Demand Gen Process

Once you have decided on the key GTM plays to focus on, you need to start executing. And that's where the demand gen process takes over. While a detailed description of this process is outside the scope of this book, a short primer will be useful to better understand how this end-to-end process works.

The typical sales process for a B2B company can be broken down into a four-step interactive undertaking. The marketing demand gen team and its activities span the first two steps. It is responsible for providing MQLs to sales. The sales team will then create targetable opportunities and move them through the sales process. Finally, the sales team will convert the opportunities into a closed (won or lost) deal.

The next figure provides an overview of the demand generation process and outlines the three major components of demand generation: demand capture, demand nurture and conversion, and the sales process.

Figure 6.1: Typical Demand Generation Process at B2B Companies

- **Demand Capture:** Involves gaining the interest of potential customers and adding them to your marketable database. This can involve a range of activities spanning establishing your brand proposition (such as digital ads and thought leadership content), owned and third-party events, as well as higher-funnel campaign pay-per-click (PPC) advertisements, search engine optimization (SEO), and third-party intent data.
- **Demand Nurture:** Most customers, particularly in B2B, interact with marketing content long before talking to someone on the sales team. That's why demand nurture is so crucial in demand generation marketing. Demand nurture starts with lead scoring (based on sales- and marketing-aligned definitions for what makes someone a qualified lead), a hot prospect, or a bad fit. Demand nurture typically involves creating highly targeted campaigns (using tactics that would fall in the middle or bottom of the funnel, like webinars, events, and interactive content) that address your leads' pain points and is appropriate to their stage in the sales funnel. Prospects interact with the offers and get scored accordingly.

- **Sales Qualification and Sales Process:** Once the right targets have been identified—MQLs —they are passed to the sales teams. Sales development rep teams usually handle MQLs by contacting the prospect—sometimes with account executives (AEs), other times without—and creating sales opportunities based on sales pipeline criteria (ready to buy, has enough budget, engaging with the right person, etc.). These opportunities are known as sales accepted leads (SALs). Sales account executives will create sales accepted opportunities (SAOs) and then execute the sales process on these opportunities to win the deals.
  - o Increasingly, but not always, sales development representatives (SDRs) report to the CMO so that marketing can be better measured and held accountable for the volume of sales opportunities and increasing pipeline. If a CMO cannot track a "lead" through the sales qualification process, then it's much harder to make them accountable for the downstream sales processes.

Now that we have an understanding of the typical demand generation process, let's take a closer look at a few foundational items that every demand generation team should be very familiar with.

The Buyer's Journey

When most campaign and product marketing managers (PMMs) think about the buyer's journey, they tend to consider it in three or four broad categories: awareness, consideration, decision, and, often, adoption. The portfolio and content marketing teams (see Chapter 5) will map material to each of the four stages. This is a useful way to think about how to structure content, though it is a bit overly simplistic.

The following figure depicts a representative buyer's journey.

Figure 6.2: Representative Buyer Journey of Customers

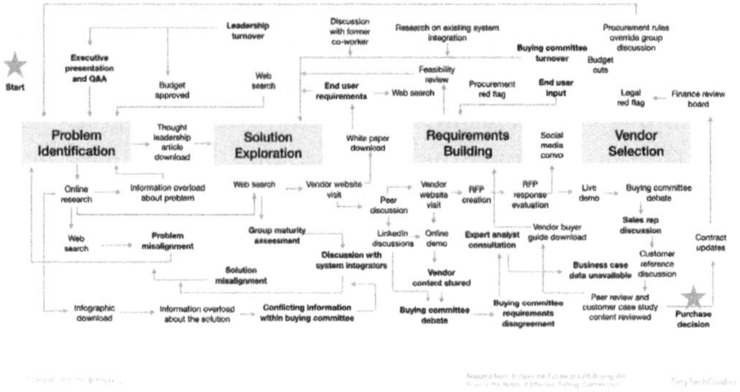

Source: Adapted from Gartner, "The B2B Buying Journey: The B2B Buying Process Has Changed, Has Your Sales Strategy?"[3]

As you can see, the buyer's journey is much more complex than the simple four-step model that most marketers use. In addition, you need to understand this intricate four-step journey across the multitude of channels (discussed below) and across buying groups (which often consist of seven to ten different individuals). No wonder B2B marketing, buying, and selling are hard!

Demand Gen Funnel

The demand generation funnel is at the heart of tracking your demand gen metrics. While the funnel varies a bit depending on the company's maturity and analytics, most companies use one (as shown below). The following figure represents a typical demand generation funnel.

Figure 6.3: Demand Generation Funnel

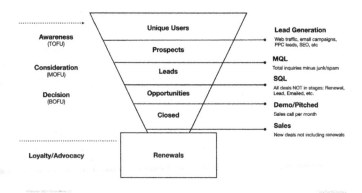

We see how users progress through the marketing funnel, which ends in closed/won business.

Demand Gen Team Areas of Focus

So how does the demand gen team execute the B2B buying process? The typical functions include:

- **Digital Marketing**: Drives frontline awareness and demand capture in many B2B enterprises, promoting products and services to other businesses and organizations through online channels and digital technologies. With the right techniques and strategies, digital marketing can improve online visibility and increase brand awareness. And in the process, more web traffic, leads, and conversions for your company.

- **Integrated Marketing (Campaigns)**: What is your demand message to prospects and customers? The core function of integrated marketing is to align channels to promote products or services in tandem, typically through a strategic campaign. Integrated marketing also works to align the primary brand message that's being delivered through marketing channels and assets.

- **Field Marketing:** Literally getting products "out in the field" in front of buying communities. Some field marketing campaigns can include trade shows, networking events, conferences, road shows, webinars, fireside chats, roundtables, and more—including virtual events (thanks, COVID).

- **Account-Based Marketing (ABM)**: ABM teams are responsible for the strategy and implementation of account-based marketing campaigns and tactics to drive pipeline from the key accounts list developed in collaboration with sales and marketing. In other words, they market directly to a business (account). These are often one-to-one or consist of only a few campaigns since the materials used are generally created for a very specific, high-potential-value account.
- **Partner Marketing**: The partner marketing team is responsible for driving awareness and demand activities with your company's partners. These can take the form of co-branded demand-generation activities, trade shows, and networking events.

Now that we know demand gen teams are often composed of digital marketing, integrated marketing, field marketing, and ABM teams, let's take a closer look at digital marketing and integrated campaigns.

Digital Marketing

When we went to business school, there was a focus on the 4Ps (see Beyond the 4Ps in Chapter 1)and trying to understand the customer's journey. This was relatively simple; the number of contact points between the customer and the business was relatively small. However, as the Internet has progressed and technology has evolved, the number of channels that customers and prospects can interact with a business has multiplied significantly.

As discussed in Chapter 3, the shifting demographics from baby boomers to millennials have changed buying habits and behaviors. Furthermore, the impact of economic uncertainty, geopolitical instabilities, and new innovative technologies have changed buying habits and behaviors across all industries and segments. Organizations can no longer operate as they have in the past. Modern, innovative organizations that figure out how to seamlessly create personalized experiences within these changing conditions will win.

In a *Harvard Business Review* (*HBR*) article, Janet Wallis, who leads EY's CMO Practice, discussed the ten new truths of marketing in a post-pandemic world.[4] We will not cover all ten here, but we've selected a few that illustrate the changing landscape in the following table.

Table 6.1: New Truths of Modern Marketing in a Post-Pandemic World

Old Truth	New Truth	Implications
You are competitive with competitors.	You are competing with the last best experience your customer had.	Customers want personalized journeys and experiences across the entire customer's journey. AI will gain prominence.
Customers hope you have what they want.	Customers expect you to have exactly what they want.	Customers demand a frictionless, connected, and relevant experience.
Customers must sit at the heart of your marketing strategy.	Customers must sit at the heart of your company and organizational structure.	Organizations need to break down organizational barriers and data silos to have a holistic view of their customers.
Relationships matter.	Relationships are everything.	Organizations are shifting from selling products to solutions. They need to understand how to create, maintain, and grow relationships in an online world (think chatbots and virtual agents).

Your brand should stand behind great products.	Your brand should stand behind great values.	It doesn't cost a lot to switch to a competitor. In addition to functional product benefits, factors like sustainability, trust, ethics, and social responsibility are more important.

Source: Adapted from Janet Balis, "10 Truths about Marketing after the Pandemic," Harvard Business Review.

McKinsey & Company highlighted the evolution in the number of channels that B2B buyers can access. You can see from the next figure that this has changed from five in 2016 to ten in 2021.[5]

Figure 6.4: Number of Channels B2B Buyers Use

Source: McKinsey.com. "The New B2B Growth Equation".[6]

Customers and prospects demanding hyper-personalized, connected experiences in the modern economy create significant implications for B2B software companies. Thus, the omnichannel strategy was born. Businesses now need to meet prospects where they are—on *their* channel of choice—with a hyper-personalized, relevant, and connected offer.

The ability to ingest, collect, analyze, and understand customer behavior in real time requires a significant investment in data and analytics infrastructure. Although this is a goal for many organizations, we have not seen an entirely connected experience in our careers. The proliferation of channels will continue to grow, and B2B companies will struggle to keep pace. But it's good for folks like us (and other data and analytic professionals—we all will have plenty of work.

Digital or Dead: The Importance of SEO

Earlier in this chapter, we discussed the buyer's journey and showed that today's sophisticated buyers do their homework before engaging a B2B company. In fact, 80 to 90 percent of B2B buyers already have a vendor in mind after their first day of research—and many millennials prefer not to engage any sales reps at all.[7] The next figure highlights the amount of time a B2B buyer spends on a supplier's website versus interacting with a sales rep.[8]

Figure 6.5: Sales Rep vs. Website Channels to Complete Buying Jobs

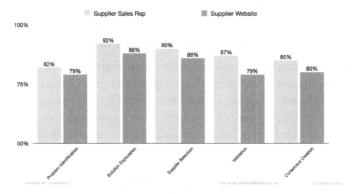

Source: 2019 Gartner B2B Buying Survey.[9]

Given these realities, it is imperative that organizations have website content that is optimized for search engines (primarily Google.com). Typically, organizations will optimize content with the search terms of interest so websites rank on the first page of Google's search results. This is known as search engine optimization (SEO). Additionally, companies will create glossary pages, which are more "informational" in nature, as Google tends to penalize vendor content in search results.

Now, one common challenge that many companies face is what keywords to select and how many to target. There's not a hard and fast limit, but a general rule of thumb is to target two or three keywords per page. You can get a sense of how many make sense for your business by doing some keyword research and understanding monthly search volumes, related terms, and so forth.

Pro Tip

Be smart about your keywords. Don't treat keywords like peanut butter. Web pages with long-tail keywords require more time and effort to maintain and update. This is what blogs and podcasts are for!

Lastly, SEO is like the ever-shifting sands. You need to create a solid set of metrics and instrumentation on the website so you can rapidly respond to changing market conditions.

What Do Digital Marketing Professionals Do?

Now that we understand the importance of digital marketing, let's look at some of the tactics that are included in digital marketing.

- **Search Engine Optimization (SEO)**: The process of adding keywords and glossary pages to your website to rank within major Internet search engines to increase traffic. Many B2B businesses optimize for Google, which accounts for 92 percent of global search traffic worldwide.[10]
- **Search Engine Marketing (SEM)**: Using paid online advertising to find users searching for specific keywords relevant to your product or brand. These typically include both display and text ads.
- **Pay-Per-Click (PPC)**: Online payment method where a business pays for ads when someone clicks on them. Unfortunately, there are a lot of bots that click things, which runs up the bill for companies.

- **Social Media Marketing (SMM)**: Using social media channels like Twitter, LinkedIn, Facebook, TikTok, and other channels to promote products or services. This may also include B2B marketing influencers.
- **Email Marketing:** As part of the demand generation and campaign strategy, you can send relevant content to prospects via email.
- **Affiliate Marketing:** Revenue-sharing, pay-per-sale business model within a common network.
- **Content Marketing:** Publishing text, audio, and video materials. This may also include sponsored content on websites like Forbes, as well as blogs, how-to videos, product tours, ROI calculators, economic impact studies, and customer stories.
- **Influencer Marketing:** Working with influencers to talk directly or indirectly about your product or service.
- **Marketing Automation:** Programs that automatically run in the background to "guide" the prospect along in a buyer's journey. A common CTA for software products is a free trial.
- **Content Syndication**: A company's content is published on a third-party website. Although this tends to get individuals into the marketing funnel, the quality of the leads is quite low.

As you can see, with so many channels the possibilities are endless. We expand on a few of these in various chapters throughout this book.

Fix Your Website

Your website is the company's storefront. It should encapsulate everything from brand to portfolio marketing. It is commonly used for lead generation activities and acts as the focal point for product-led growth (PLG) activities. If you recall, 80 to 90 percent of buyers conduct research on a vendor's website before contacting them.

"The hardest part of B2B solutions isn't selling them, but buying them," says Brent Adamson, principal executive advisor at Gartner. "Today's buying journey has effectively reached a tipping point where it's become nearly unnavigable without a significant amount of help."[11]

Whatever the reason, many B2B companies have outdated, ineffective web pages with layout templates that prohibit the telling of a compelling story—the navigation is often befuddling and the content is stale and outdated. Your website should be simple and have content that informs buyers and makes it as easy as possible to find relevant, contextualized information applicable to their needs.

Here are some average stats for homepages:
- Session Length: ~1.5 to 2 minutes
- Page Views: ~2
- Unique Page Views: ~1.5
- Bounce Rate: ~70 percent
- Conversion Rate: ~2–3 percent

What do those stats mean? That you have about two minutes—and two pages—to get your point across.

One of the high-tech companies we worked for embarked on a project to redesign its homepage. This is never a fun task in a B2B company—there are a lot of opinions about where content should be, the page load speeds were low, conversion rates were dismal, and content was stale. Different executive leaders wanted different types of content; eventually, it was a "herding cats" scenario.
Rather than going through another endless bout of meetings and opinions, we took a metrics-based approach. Using heat maps and software that tracks user behaviors, we ended up removing about 75 percent of the content and keeping the most relevant content—based on user behavior, not in-office opinion.

Our recommendations for a good homepage:
- Keep it simple. Have an engaging banner with a simple message and design.
- Keep text jargon-free and to the point.
- Optimize for mobile.
- Be prescriptive about where you want the user to go.
- Make the navigation simple.
- Ensure content is snackable and in the correct format for your target audience.
- Personalize the experience as much as possible.

ROI of Digital Marketing

Now that we've discussed the details of digital marketing, what is its ROI ? The next figure highlights the fact that the more digital channels a company invests in, the faster it tends to grow.

Figure 6.6: ROI of Digital Marketing Initiatives

Market share gainers, by number of channels engaged

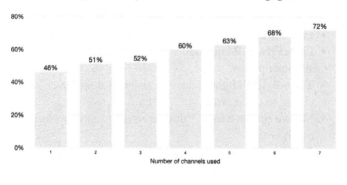

Source: Arora, Harrison, Plotkin, Magni, and Stanley. "The New B2B Growth Equation."[12]

Counting the Beans (Attribution Models)

Now, one of the challenges of modern marketing is marketing getting "credit" for the pipeline that is generated. Enter the bean counting—otherwise known as marketing attribution. There are various attribution models as identified in the following figure.

Figure 6.7: Marketing Attribution Models

Attribution Models

- **First Touch**: All value is assigned to the first touch point.
- **Last Touch**: All value is assigned to the last touch point.
- **Linear (Non-Weighted)**: Values are assigned equally across all touch points.
- **Time-Based**: Higher values are assigned at the touch points closest to conversion.
- **Measurement-Based**: Values assigned to most measurable touch points.
- **Position-Based**: Values assigned to first and last touch points.

What portion of the pipeline should be delivered by marketing? The numbers vary depending on the maturity and typical annual contract value (ACV) of the deals: earlier-stage companies depend much more on marketing pipeline while smaller deal-size companies (sub $10–15,000 average selling price) also expect a more marketing-driven pipeline. On average, in a modern B2B marketing organization, marketing-driven demand generation activities should account for 30 percent of the generated pipeline. Sales, partner, and customer success channels typically deliver the rest.

Sourced versus Influenced Pipeline

Many marketing organizations spend significant time trying to understand the right mix of sourced versus influenced pipelines. Before we discuss this in detail, let's begin with a few definitions:

- **Sourced Pipeline:** Generated by initiatives—campaigns or events—driven by the marketing department. These sales opportunities wouldn't exist without the marketing department.
- **Influenced Pipeline:** Marketing activities that help convert an existing contact that becomes a qualified lead (QL). Imagine if a prospect is already working with sales; the prospect then visits your website and downloads a few marketing assets. In this case, marketing is helping to move the engagement forward; hence, the pipeline created is called influenced pipeline.

Understanding different types of pipelines is necessary for understanding which tactics, programs, and campaigns are influencing your deals. This way, you can double down on the ones that are working and either refine or remove noneffective campaigns. The problem with how organizations count the beans is that it becomes a game of "who gets credit for what." You've heard the adage "measurement drives behavior." Well, it certainly did for the companies we worked for.

One of the issues with this measurement system is that it's more "inward" focused and does not put the prospective buyers, and their experiences, at the center of the process. Decisions are made on what content to gate (i.e., put behind a registration form) and which to make available for free based on attribution models. Most organizations are only able to use attribution models for content elements that are gated. How about the social media post that a lead saw on LinkedIn—how do you count that? How about blogs, website visits, YouTube videos, thought leadership articles, and so forth? Because it is very difficult to count them, they are generally just ignored by most companies.

The other challenge is that, when a buying group consists of seven to ten individuals who each might use ten different channels (with over twenty interactions each), how does a marketing organization account for that?

> Buying has changed, but measurement hasn't. Buyers are engaging in more buying interactions than ever before, and buying groups, while always a core part of B2B buying, have been expanding. Forrester's 2021 B2B Buying Survey showed that B2B buyers engage in an average of 27 interactions over the course of a buying journey (up 93% since 2015), and 60% of B2B purchases now involve groups of four or more people. Nearly one-third of buying cycles span four or more months (compared with less than one-fifth in 2015). Yet sourcing metrics steer the conversation of impact toward which function can clearly claim responsibility for that first interaction with a buyer. A sourcing focus, while not ideal when buying was simpler, isn't holding up in the face of more complex buying dynamics.

We've seen no evidence that organizations with high rates of marketing sourcing experience higher win rates, bigger deal sizes, or greater cost efficiency across the revenue engine. Simply put, higher rates of sourcing don't equate to more revenue.[13]

Now, to measure marketing effectiveness, Forrester has developed a concept called revenue lift. This essentially tries to account for marketing's impact by setting a threshold on the number of interactions and then calculating the associated lift with that. We do not have experience with this methodology, so we will move on but wanted to acknowledge that it's early in adoption.

Demand Generation

The demand generation teams are a busy bunch. We had a chance to speak with Rupa Menon, a senior director of demand generation:

> Demand gen professionals essentially work to create a smooth and seamless buyer's journey for customers and prospects. This is done through crafting a series of programs, tactics, and content that "touch" the buyer in various stages and through the various watering holes that they visit to consume content. They need to do all of this while keeping a goal in mind—creating qualified leads that convert to opportunities which eventually create bookings for the business.

The demand generation team is generally involved in the following activities:

Planning and Strategy

- Lead demand and lead generation planning, including the overall strategy of demand creation, nurturing, and lead scoring.
- Setting up new and nurtured lead generation goals and forecasts.
- Determining the budget spend priorities.

Operationalize

- Developing campaign strategies that leverage the full scope of marketing programs, including online, tradeshow, events, email nurturing programs, telemarketing, advertising, etc.
- Working with the marketing team to develop targeted content assets for prospecting, nurturing, and converting.
- Managing the lead qualification process using predictive lead scoring and refining end-to-end campaign and lead management processes.
- Enabling and training the sales development reps (SDRs) and business development reps (BDRs) about in-market programs and follow-up.

Measure, Optimize, and Refine

- Measuring overall results against plans and analyzing performance against lead and other marketing goals to continually drive marketing ROI.
- Providing periodic reports to senior leadership for KPIs (leads, opportunities, ROI, etc.).

Day in the Life of a Demand Gen Professional

When we asked Menon what a day in the life of a campaign manager looked like, she shared the following activities:

- Establishing campaign foundation with buyer need-based use-case campaigns and crafting of buyer's journey. Identify gaps in content or program inventory.
- Programming metrics and goal tracking via website visits, webinar attendees, email metrics, search, and social media metrics, etc.
- Aligning with sales goals.
- Positioning upcoming events with pre- and post-event activation strategies.
- Ensuring every prospect's activity is followed by a nurture sequence.

- Understanding the persona demographics and firmographics to plan programs that attract them to solution areas.
- Planning engagement with key influencers and content syndication vendors.
- Emailing cold prospects weekly with key messages.
- Preparing social promos in parallel with campaign activation.
- Tracking KPIs on a weekly, monthly, and quarterly basis with MQLs, SALs, sales qualified leads (SQL), opportunity pipeline, and marketing-originated bookings (MOBs).
- Ensuring sales is aware of all campaigns in the market—weekly sync calls, monthly campaign update newsletter, and participation in calls with the core and extended teams.
- Organizing "ask me anything" (AMA) workshops for sales to chat with campaign managers about current and future campaigns.
- Working with product managers and PMMs on upcoming product launches and creating tiger teams to support them and for upcoming AR reports.
- Partnering with thought leadership team on blog series, including highlighting the main campaign themes and choosing the right CTAs.
- A/B testing CTAs on prominent pages on the website.
- Creating SEO /glossary pages and reference center pages created in tandem with the content team and PMMs. These should all have relevant CTA as hooks for customers and prospects.
- Ensuring that the community pages have the right CTAs to capture lead information.
- Working with the website team and MOPs on auto-MQL programs (demos, contact us, trial, and chatbot) and ensuring that there are no leakages.
- Doing a monthly check on program ROI and calculating pipeline return multiplier from programs in market.
- Reviewing ad copy, keywords, and offers for paid media ads (and keep an eye on CPL and cost per acquisition (CPA)).

- Communicating with the content team weekly to ensure that content launches (in-house and third-party) are on track with an integrated promotional plan.
- Drafting with MOPs email and nurture metrics and understanding data and results from A/B tests.
- Reviewing closed-won and closed-lost deals weekly and understand the lead journey to make better decisions.

Who Makes the Best Demand Gen Professionals?

Menon looks for the following qualities in a demand gen (campaign) manager:

- Acts as a mini CMO for campaigns.
- Strategic mindset, data-driven, flawless execution, and operates with a sense of urgency.
- Acts as an owner and understands "we win as a team."
- Sees ROI as a key metric.
- Effective communicator, both verbally and in writing.
- Collaborates efficiently with cross-team functions.
- Self-critical and always finds room for improvement and growth.
- Constantly optimizing.
- Flexibility to adapt.
- Problem-solving and creative thinking.
- Strong attention to detail.
- Interpersonal skills.
- Project management.
- Passionate thinker and doer.

These are great qualities to look for when you're hiring your next demand-generation professional.

KPIs for Demand Generation

- **Pipeline**: The most important metric for demand gen teams, pipeline represents the true contribution of marketing to the overall business.

- **Visit-to-Lead Conversion:** Too often, marketers aggressively focus on the number of new marketing-qualified leads generated through a campaign. While this is a critical metric, it ignores the middle-of-the-funnel touchpoints and metrics that determine how effectively your organization is providing relevant content, nurturing relationships, and passing qualified leads to sales.
- **MQLs to SQLs to Meetings to Conversions**: Building on conversions in general, brands may also want to track things like how many MQLs convert to SQLs and how many SQLs book meetings—and then how many of those meetings lead to closed deals. These insights can inform your organization about any weaknesses within the funnel and any areas that can be improved.
- **Cost Per Lead (CPL)**: Calculated by dividing paid media costs by the total number of leads generated from marketing efforts. This metric can reveal how much you're spending on average per campaign, persona, or channel. The ideal varies considerably by industry, though B2Bs can expect to pay a lot more to bring new leads into the pipeline, particularly when using highly-targeted paid channels.
- **Cost Per (Customer) Acquisition**: This is total marketing spend—salaries, commissions, and bonuses divided by the number of new customers—and it can make or break your business. Simply put, if customer acquisition costs are higher than the average customer lifetime value, there's no way an organization will be able to turn a profit. Tracking this metric can serve as a starting point for a deeper dive into suboptimal marketing programs. It serves as a red flag that, when taken seriously, can help fine-tune campaign goals, strategies, and targeting.
- **Closed MQL Percentage**: MQLs qualify for nurturing and/or retargeting based on data that aligns with a certain set of criteria (i.e., these leads are likely to convert sometime in the future). In the context of a demand generation program, MQLs should be tracked using closed-loop analytics, with

marketing receiving feedback to inform their strategy moving forward. Tracking the number of MQLs that convert and then reporting back to marketing allows you to ensure the right people are being targeted on the right platforms.

- **Average Deal Size (ADS)**: Calculating this is pretty straightforward: it's the average value of each new deal closed during the sales cycle. Depending on what you sell, deal size might correlate with customer lifetime value (i.e., SaaS products billed monthly or annually, subscriptions, or long-term contracts). ADS plays a major role in forecasting by allowing teams to accurately project revenue, set quotas, and manage the pipeline sustainably. Additionally, looking at the average deal size by persona can provide information about which accounts a company should target to maximize revenue.

- **Customer Lifetime Value (CLV)**: Represents the total amount a customer is likely to spend over the duration of the relationship with your brand. This metric offers an inside look into the ability to continue delivering a great experience to customers after a deal closes.

- **Return on Marketing Investment (ROMI)**: Calculated differently depending on the organization. We've seen it as a marketing-sourced pipeline and marketing-influenced pipeline divided by marketing expenses. Tracking this ratio can help illustrate how marketing investments influence revenue.

- **Web Traffic Sources:** This can indicate your website's overall health. Traffic sources are generally measured in terms of direct traffic, search traffic, and referral traffic. If traffic sources are increasing, it is generally a good sign that a website provides useful information and is optimized for SEO. The brand team also uses this KPI to understand its effectiveness.

Now, there are many other KPIs tracked by marketing teams, including page views, click-through rates, return visitors, etc., but we find the above list closer to the business outcomes campaign managers are trying to achieve.

Practical Advice and Next Steps

- While DG teams can focus on many metrics (as seen above), pipeline is the most important— pipeline, pipeline, pipeline. While DG teams like to showcase other metrics, it is the ONLY metric that truly matters (though closed revenue is important too).

- Pipeline, as well as other marketing metrics, can be seasonal and vary by month or quarter. It can also be very lopsided, as the enterprise may see significant pipeline growth in certain quarters. For example, the Europe, Middle East, and Africa (EMEA) pipeline is usually low from July-Aug because most of the EMEA GTM is on vacation around these times. Additionally, the later part of the quarter (as sales inputs high-fidelity opportunities into the CRM system) also creates lumpiness. It's important for marketing teams to track year-over-year (YoY) comparisons and trends as a benchmark (by week into quarter), besides tracking absolute goal attainment.

- Due to the proliferation of channels, B2B organizations should make significant investments in data and analytic infrastructure. The ability to understand your customers and deliver hyper-personalized offers depends on it.

- Consider how you count the beans in your organization and the behavior it drives. Is your organization customer-centric or inward-focused?

- Fix your homepage—it's your storefront. You have one chance to make an impact in less than two minutes. Create snackable content and be prescriptive about where site visitors should go.

Summary

- Demand generation teams work with various groups across the organization to define GTM market motions, also known as sales plays.
- Most organizations look at metrics through the demand gen funnel, which starts with responses and moves to MQLs, SQLs, and then closed/won business.
- There is a myriad of marketing metrics that marketing organizations track, but the only ones that truly matter are pipeline and closed/won business.
- Buyers today demand that you meet them on their channel of choice and expect you to deliver connected, hyper-personalized experiences.
- A majority of research is conducted by a buying committee of seven to ten individuals.
- Marketing attribution is a big topic and drives organizations to create content and activities that stakeholders can get "credit" for, which drives behavior optimized for measurement and not results.

Chapter 6 References

1 Turner, Jordan. "What Marketing Budgets Look Like in 2022." Gartner. June 6, 2022. https://www.gartner.com/en/articles/what-marketing-budgets-look-like-in-2022.

2 Gartner Glossary. "Demand Generation." Gartner. Accessed December 29, 2022. https://www.gartner.com/en/marketing/glossary/demand-generation.

3 "The B2B Buying Journey: The B2B Buying Process Has Changed, Has Your Sales Strategy?" Gartner. Accessed April 23, 2023. https://www.gartner.com/en/sales/insights/b2b-buying-journey.

4 Balis, Janet. "10 Truths about Marketing after the Pandemic." *Harvard Business Review*. March 10, 2021. https://hbr.org/2021/03/10-truths-about-marketing-after-the-pandemic.

5 Arora, Arun, Liz Harrison, Candace Lun Plotkin, Max Magni,

and Jennifer Stanley. "The New B2B Growth Equation." McKinsey & Company. February 23, 2022. https://www.mckinsey.com/capabilities/growth-marketing-and-sales/our-insights/the-new-b2b-growth-equation.

[6] Arora et al. "The New B2B Growth Equation."

[7] Sherrard, Saber, Rishi Dave, and Mollie Parker MacGregor. "What B2Bs Need to Know about Their Buyers." *Harvard Business Review*. September 20, 2022. https://hbr.org/2022/09/what-b2bs-need-to-know-about-their-buyers.

[8] "The B2B Buying Journey." Gartner.

[9] "The B2B Buying Journey." Gartner.

[10] Emnace, Hazel. "25 Essential Google Search Statistics." Fit Small Business, March 8, 2023. https://fitsmallbusiness.com/google-search-statistics/.

[11] Adamson, Brent. "Win More B2B Sales Deals: How Sales Delivers More Value to Today's Buyers." Gartner, 2018. https://emtemp.gcom.cloud/ngw/globalassets/en/sales-service/documents/trends/win-more-b2b-sales-deals.pdf.

[12] Arora et al. "The New B2B Growth Equation."

[13] Graber, Ross. "B2B Marketers: It's Time to Ditch Sourcing Metrics." Forrester. March 11, 2022. https://www.forrester.com/blogs/b2b-marketers-its-time-to-ditch-sourcing-metrics/.

CHAPTER 7

Marketing Operations

What Are Marketing Operations?

Now that we have an understanding of the different functional areas in a modern B2B marketing organization, we turn our attention to the marketing operations team, also known as the MOPs team. It typically owns the systems that automate many of the marketing processes, including email sends, drip campaigns, nurture campaigns, and others. The MOPs team is also usually responsible for keeping track of all marketing metrics (see Counting the Beans) reported to the CMO and board of directors.

Fundamentally, the MOPs team is the group responsible for operationalizing all of the marketing content —ensuring the right content is distributed to the right persona, in the right channel, and at the right stage of the buyer's journey. It is important to have a strong MOPs team closely aligned with the sales operations teams so that, together, they can help the organization implement GTM program plays.

Why Is Marketing Ops Important?

Without a marketing operations team, you will not be effective or efficient in delivering your GTM campaigns (see Chapter 6). The team helps achieve economies of scale with your campaigns and typically owns the systems, data, CRM, and project coordination across the organization. It helps develop best practices and ensures you don't target the same individual too frequently with different and conflicting campaigns and messages.

Simply put, MOPs enable the entire marketing organization by providing the right process, tech, and people skills to meet the outcomes of the organization. The next figure illustrates how process, team, and tech come together within marketing.

Figure 7.1: Interlock Between Processes, Team, and Technology

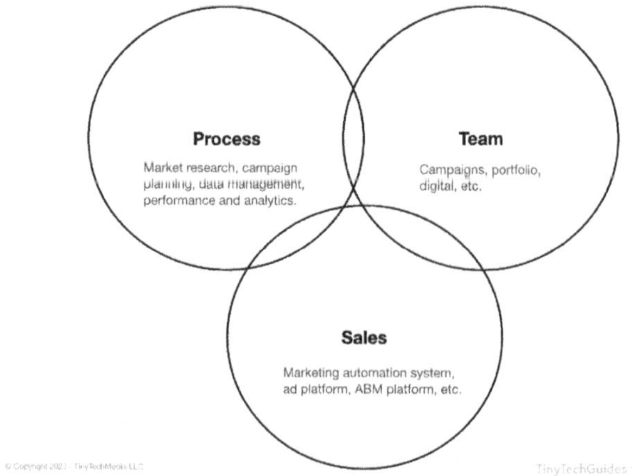

Process
Market research, campaign planning, data management, performance and analytics.

Team
Campaigns, portfolio, digital, etc.

Sales
Marketing automation system, ad platform, ABM platform, etc.

© Copyright 2023 - TinyTechMedia LLC

TinyTechGuides™

What Does Marketing Ops Do?

The core responsibility of the marketing ops is to ensure that the marketing team is functioning efficiently and executing with agility in support of marketing goals and strategy. This team leads and orchestrates the development, alignment, and optimization of all cross-functional processes, infrastructure, and operating models within overall marketing.

The MOPs team is generally responsible for the following:

- **Systems**: Orchestrating and implementing the best automation systems and software to support marketing campaigns (e.g., determining how and where your team tracks and targets leads). It is also responsible for the analytics engine that provides visibility regarding marketing performance (these technologies are proliferating, with a recent survey suggesting that teams can have between four and twenty tools—which is a lot to juggle).
- **Onboarding**: Responsible for onboarding team members in the use of marketing technology, managing seats, enablement, and monitoring usage.
- **Analytics and Metrics**: Using data to help marketers determine who their audience is, how to best reach it, and assess the performance of past campaigns.
- **Email and CRM Processes**: Maintaining the infrastructure to communicate with customers, often putting in a series of rules regarding how many times a prospective customer can receive marketing communication. After all, if you send out too many emails, the prospect is more likely to unsubscribe.
- **Rules and Regulations**: Generally responsible for ensuring all of the appropriate rules and regulations like the General Data Protection Regulation (GDPR) and California Consumer Privacy Act (CCPA) are followed.
- **Project Management**: Determining and documenting processes that everyone should follow to achieve all of the above.
- **Contact Database Health:** Usually maintaining the underlying database of customers and prospects that marketing teams target. The MOPs team is charged with ensuring that good quality data is available—with the right level of detail and granularity so target segments and user personas can be reached.

Without a MOPs team, things tend to descend into chaos because there is no coordination across the different marketing teams.

What Makes a Good Marketing Ops Leader?

The scientific aspect of marketing has exponentially increased over the last five years or so. While there is still an appreciation for the "art" of marketing, the tangible, quantitative aspect of it is what makes CMOs high-visibility, but often vulnerable, executives (see Chapter 1). This environment makes the market ops leader (and team) very critical partners to the CMO and marketing leadership team.

A good marketing ops leader is a strong, collaborative partner to the CMO and a trusted advisor to the chief revenue officer (CRO) and VP of sales, etc., a dynamic that often runs through relationships with sales ops. (As mentioned in Chapter 1, it is increasingly the case that the CMO works for the CRO.) The marketing ops leader will know the data inside out and use that knowledge to establish credible, practical alignment between sales and marketing. Only data that is understood—and believed by both sales and marketing executives—will work. Anything less makes the CMO extremely vulnerable.

The MOPs leader is also responsible for ensuring that standardized processes—everything from annual planning and budget management to a regular view/discussion of the metrics that matter—are executed in an organized and repeatable fashion. Good MOPs leaders are strategic in their thinking and partnership with the CMO and in ensuring that their organizations are pragmatic and excellent executors.

What Do Marketing Ops Professionals Do?

Marketing ops professionals generally have a strong background in systems, data, and analytics. After all, they are implementing the strategy and GTM motions that your organization is pursuing. Their key activities include:

System and Data Management

- Overseeing the marketing technology infrastructure, including implementation, integration, feature enhancements, and usability.
- Implementing privacy regulations across all marketing systems.
- Creating scalable and repeatable processes for everyone.
- Building automated processes to reduce manual work so marketers can focus on creative efforts.

Email and CRM Management

- Monitoring email deliverability and making recommendations based on performance (this responsibility may be shared with demand gen teams).
- Managing email data for audience segmentation and optimizing email campaigns for critical stages of the customer's journey (this responsibility may be shared with demand gen teams).
- Controlling CRM data for things like lead scoring.
- Collaborating with engineering and data teams to fix bugs or implement new features in CRM, email, or other marketing automation tools.
- Setting up CRM and email automation to personalize email campaigns at scale.
- Maintaining email subscription and exclusion lists.

Project Management

- Providing training, user access, and provision of internal marketing tools.
- Developing workflows and best practices to help other teams execute projects.

Day in the Life of a Marketing Ops Professional

The marketing operations manager works with numerous stakeholders across the entire organization and responsibilities include:

- Creating marketing attribution models to track marketing efficacy.
- Developing reports and analytics that track marketing performance including campaign performance, website performance, and digital performance.
- Writing reports and dashboards for quarterly business reviews (QBRs), board meetings, etc.
- Facilitate business-oriented discussion on marketing metrics across the organization.
- Designing, running, and optimizing marketing campaigns (in partnership with demand gen).
- Onboarding, training, and enabling marketers on the marketing technology (MarTech) stack.
- Researching and recommending new marketing technologies for inclusion in the MarTech stack.
- Integrating MarTech stack with business systems.
- Building, maintaining, monitoring, and improving marketing database quality.
- Monitoring the technical performance of marketing technology.
- Conducting data privacy, compliance, and security reviews of MarTech products and processes.

Who Makes a Good Marketing Ops Professional?

In our experience, the best marketing operations professionals exhibit the following qualities.

- Good understanding of high-performing marketing technology stack (example technologies like Marketo, Google Analytics, Salesforce, Zoom, ZoomInfo, ON24, Cvent, Monday.com, etc.).

- Effective marketing reporting and analysis (example analytics systems include Tableau, Power BI, Excel, etc.).
- Passionate about data and what it tells the org about what is working and what is not.
- Provides effective data management within the marketing automation and CRM systems.
- Defines and supports the appropriate processes to streamline the delivery of marketing programs and tasks.
- Supports planning and budgeting cycles (quarterly, half-year, annually).
- Works with marketing leadership to support the evolution of marketing function and structure.

KPIs to Measure Effectiveness

In the end, marketing operations' KPIs, as with the rest of the organization, should map to business outcomes. Rather than using different KPIs, we will include metrics that are unique to MOPs teams.

- **On-Time Analysis and Reporting of the Marketing KPIs:** Reporting of goals and metrics to all stakeholders. This is usually delivered on a weekly or bi-weekly basis to executive teams as well as other GTM stakeholders.
- **Developing and Documenting Marketing Plan:** While all marketing teams contribute to the strategic marketing plan, the marketing ops team generally owns the plan and socializes the plan with stakeholders.
- **Marketing Database Quality Health:** Identify marketable (right ICP/title/roles) and invalid (bounced, duplicates, unsubscribed) contacts in the database and ensure that the GTM team has good coverage to meet MQL/pipeline needs.
- **Compliance with Regulations**: Ensure that the right compliance requirements (GDPR, CCPA, Payment Card Industry (PCI), etc.) are implemented in all marketing systems.

- **Automation Effectiveness**: While marketing teams have many processes, MOPs can track the percentage of critical processes that are automated/codified to drive effectiveness within the marketing teams.
- **Metric Dashboard Usability and Accessibility**: As the KPI implies, no operational dashboard (or data, for that matter) is useful unless the right folks are getting access to the reports and can use them effectively in their work. Marketing ops teams should pay close attention to the daily/weekly/monthly active viewers and users for the reports they create. The reports or dashboards that do get many eyeballs should be constantly improved, while the others should be mothballed (or changed).

Practical Advice and Next Steps

- Visibility into everything all the time. Hold weekly meetings to show full marketing visibility. Make sure to include sales and executive leadership in those sessions.
- Always know your data. Nothing tarnishes the credibility of the MOPs leader or team like the data being "wrong" or a lack of understanding about what the data is saying.
- Establish a project management office (PMO) and balance process with agility.

Summary

- MOPs is responsible for the technology stack used to automate processes and operationalize GTM strategy.
- MOPs is responsible for defining and implementing best practices across the organization, especially between sales and marketing.
- MOPs is responsible for the data literacy of the marketing organization. It also needs an in-depth understanding of the data and what it implies for the marketing organization.

CHAPTER 8

Marketing Benchmarks

What Are Typical Marketing Benchmarks?

Data is the lingua franca, or common language, of marketing. Marketing has data galore—budget, pipeline, website, campaign, email response rate, social media engagement, and conversion data (just to name a few). Therefore, every company needs answers to the following questions and benchmarks:

- What does the typical marketing budget look like?
    - How do you allocate this budget between the various marketing teams?
    - How do you allocate this budget to the various marketing programs you run?
- What programs work?
    - What tactics do marketers use successfully?
    - What are the typical conversions of these tactics?
    - How many marketers should be assigned to these programs?
- How do you plan an overall marketing model that meets the requirements of a business?

In this chapter, we will provide some data points and benchmarks based on our experience. But a caveat first: There is no such thing as "typical." Your benchmarks are dependent on many factors highly specific to the company and its GTM motion. Some of these include:

- **Overall Goal of the Marketing Function**: Are you an early-stage company with little to no market awareness? In a competitive market that requires getting ahead of the competitors? Or a later-stage company with a stable sales team that is trying to build demand for it to pursue?
- **Go-to-Market Motion**: Are you running a bottoms-up motion and trying to reach out to large volumes of practitioners, or a top-down motion primarily focused on economic buyers?
- **Ideal Customer Profiles**: Are they digitally savvy folks (developers, analysts, or cloud practitioners) or do you typically find them at physical events like trade shows, etc.?
- **Company Goals**: Are you trying to drive awareness or brand?

Since there are so many caveats to these benchmarks, we will provide some data points from our real-world experience to show how these data points adhere (or differ) for actual companies.

Why Are Benchmarks Important?

Since there is so much data involved with marketing, understanding relevant benchmarks helps an organization understand its effectiveness and any gaps that a function may have relative to competitors. If you can perform above industry benchmarks, then you can effectively outperform industry competitors. Effective benchmarks allow:

- Understanding marketing effectiveness and uncovering any existing gaps, which are the areas your company should focus on for improvement.
- Better ascertaining competitors so they can be more effectively competed against.
- Setting goals and performance expectations that the company can measure and track.

- Correcting and adapting a course to evolving and changing market conditions.

Now that we appreciate the importance of benchmarks, let's examine the most important ones.

Five Marketing Benchmarks You Should Understand

Top-Down Marketing Spend

One way to approximate the marketing budget is to calculate it as a portion of the overall enterprise spend. According to Deloitte's Annual CMO Survey, marketing will comprise roughly 13.6 percent of a company's total budget in 2023.[1] The following figure represents marketing budgets as a percentage of overall company budgets, consistent with Gartner's budget research that was highlighted in Chapter 1.

Figure 8.1: Marketing Budget as Percentage of Overall Company Budget

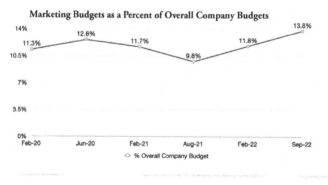

Source: Moorman, Christine. "The CMO Survey: Marketing in a Post COVID Era."[2]

How does marketing utilize these budgets? In general, most marketing teams split this budget equally across programs, tools, systems, and people. After setting aside about 20 percent for technology, the 50-50 allocation of programs to people makes sense as a heuristic for most organizations—after all, if you don't have the right people ideating, executing, and optimizing programs, you are not going to get much value from them.

What works in the real world?

In many of the companies we have worked at, the marketing budget is usually around 10 to 12 percent of the organization's ARR. While this budget can be higher in earlier-stage companies, and sometimes as high as 20 percent in well-funded ones, the budget usually settles into the 10 percent ARR range as the company matures.

In terms of program-to-people spend, we have generally seen an equal (50/50) split as a good starting point. These allocations can vary by priority—some companies we have been at have chosen to focus on brand building, and thus allocated approximately 60 to 65 percent of the budget on such programs, while others have focused on digital demand programs (which can soak up a lot of budget spend). We recommend that enterprises not invest beyond 60 to 65 percent for programs or people. After all, not having the right set of marketing resources (i.e., people to actually shepherd the programs effectively), is a surefire way of ensuring less-than-optimal execution and ultimate program KPI failures.

Functional Spending Allocation within Marketing

Now that you understand the marketing budget envelope, how is it allocated amongst the various marketing teams?

If you recall from Chapter 1, the Gartner survey "What Marketing Budgets Look Like in 2022" highlights the top priorities for CMOs.[3]

1. Campaign Creation and Management: 10.1 percent
2. Brand Strategy and Activation: 9.7 percent
3. Marketing Operations: 9.6 percent
4. Demand Generation/Sales Enablement: 9.5 percent
5. Digital Commerce: 9.4 percent

What works in the real world?

A practical allocation we have seen in some of the companies includes the following across various marketing functions:

- DG Program Budget (campaign, execution, website, etc.): 50 percent
- Brand Strategy (including AR /PR): 10–15 percent
- Content: 10 percent
- Marketing Operations and Systems: 10 percent
- Other Programs: 5–10 percent

Since demand gen usually makes up ~50 percent of marketing program spend, let's look at the allocation of this budget. We generally see two key demand gen channels:

- **Online Programs**: Paid channels like search/SEM, social and display ads, content syndication channels, ABM programs, and unpaid channels like SEO content, email marketing, etc.
- **Offline Programs**: Events like owned and sponsored conferences, field activities, field ABM programs, etc.

Setting the spend allocation for demand programs is both an art and a science. We have generally seen companies over-invest in what works and experiment with new campaign tactics. The general rule of thumb is to allocate a 50/50 split between online and offline channels.

Marketing Pipeline Model and Contribution

One of the core goals of marketing is to create demand and pipeline for the enterprise. What pipeline should an enterprise expect from marketing? This is very dependent on the maturity of the company (i.e., ARR or revenue), ACV (i.e., the average deal size), and the complexity of the product or solution.

Let's look at company maturity first.

In mature enterprises (over $1 billion ARR), the typical pipeline contribution to sales includes:

- Sales (outbound): 40 percent
- Marketing: 30 percent

- Channel: 30 percent

In earlier-stage enterprises, especially ones with lower ACV deal sizes ($20 to $200 million ARR), these ratios could change significantly.
- Sales (outbound): 45–50 percent
- Marketing: 30–50 percent
- Channel: 5–10 percent

What works in the real world?

Our experience is that most enterprises expect 25 to 30 percent pipeline contribution from marketing. This goes up as the ACV deal size reduces (that is, the lower the deal size, the higher the marketing contribution), but marketing seldom originates more than 35 to 40 percent of the enterprise pipeline.

Marketing Conversion Benchmarks

Let's say you have allocated monies to marketing programs. And marketing produces many pipeline metrics. What does this typically look like across many of the pipeline stages? The next table illustrates the average conversion rates by type of organization and the one following highlights conversion rates per tactic.

Table 8.1: Conversion Rates by Company Size and Demand Gen Funnel

Stage of Funnel	Small Business ($1M-$10M)	Small to Midsize ($10M - $100M)	Middle Market ($100M - $1B)	Enterprise ($1B+)
Website Visitor				
Lead	2.3%	1.4%	1.2%	0.7%
MQL	37%	41%	40%	34%
SQL	32%	39%	39%	40%
Opportunity	40%	42%	46%	36%
Closed	46%	39%	35%	31%

Table 8.2: Conversion Rates Per Tactic

Stage of Funnel	SEO	PPC	LinkedIn	Email	Webinar
Website Visitor					
Lead	2.1%	0.7%	2.2%	1.3%	0.9%
MQL	41%	36%	38%	43%	44%
SQL	51%	26%	30%	46%	39%
Opportunity	49%	38%	41%	48%	42%
Closed	36%	35%	39%	32%	40%

Source: Evan Bailyn, "B2B SaaS Funnel Conversion Benchmarks."[4]

What works in the real world?

Having worked in many organizations with low-friction sales models (SaaS companies with a signup-and-try motion or on-premises software companies with a download-and-try motion), we have generally seen MQL-to-closed won ratio in the 4 to 6 percent range. The conversion rates in companies without a low-friction sales model could be lower. We have seen MQL-to-closed won conversion rates of 1 to 2 percent. Also, as a rule of thumb, the cost per MQL is around $500 to $700.

A Bottom-Up Marketing Budget Supporting Enterprise ARR

Let's put it all together and arrive at a marketing budget and pipeline model that delivers an enterprise goal.

Assume Acme Corporation has an ARR of $100 million and is growing at 50 percent YoY. The average deal size of Acme is $50,000 ACV. The following table shows the Acme model for marketing budget and conversion. We have also provided cells where you can enter your own data to arrive at a marketing budget.

Table 8.3: Worksheet to Calculate Marketing Budget

KPI	Acme Metrics	Your Metrics	Notes/Assumptions
ARR	$100M		Current top line
YoY growth	$50M		Annual ARR growth
Marketing Contribution	$17M		30% of ARR comes from marketing pipeline
# of won deals	340		Closed won/ACV, assuming $50K ACV
MQLs needed	6800		Deals/.05 (assumes 5% MQL -> closed conversion)
Marketing program spend	$3.4M		Assumes $500 per MQL
Marketing people spend	$3.4M		On average, People/ Program = 50/50 of total marketing budget
Total marketing Spend (Budget)	$6.8M		

Practical Advice and Next Steps

- Understand the benchmarks in your industry and use them to gauge how competitive and effective your company is.
- As you begin the budgeting process, make sure your organization is in alignment with our guidance above.

Summary

- Benchmarks can help companies better understand their competitive position within the industry.
- The top five benchmarks you need to be aware of are:
  o Top-down marketing spend
  o Functional spending allocation
  o Marketing pipeline model and contribution

o Marketing conversion benchmarks
o A bottom-up approach to creating a marketing budget

Chapter 8 References

[1] Moorman, Christine. "The CMO Survey: Marketing in a Post COVID Era." The CMO Survey. September, 2022. https://cmosurvey.org/results/september-2022/.

[2] Moorman. "The CMO Survey."

[3] Turner, Jordan. 2022. "What Marketing Budgets Look Like in 2022." Gartner. June 6, 2022. https://www.gartner.com/en/articles/what-marketing-budgets-look-like-in-2022.

[4] Bailyn, Evan. "B2B SaaS Funnel Conversion Benchmarks." First Page Sage. February 24, 2021. https://firstpagesage.com/seo-blog/b2b-saas-funnel-conversion-benchmarks-fc.

CHAPTER 9

High-Performance Marketing

What Is High-Performance Marketing?

Building and creating high-performance marketing function is the dream of every CMO and marketing leader. But what does it mean? This is not something that happens overnight—creating a high-performance marketing culture takes foresight, planning, patience, and persistence.

We believe that there are two skill sets that separate top-performing teams from average ones:

- **Hard Skills**: These include the actual goals, processes, and techniques needed to meet the priorities of the organization.
- **Soft Skills**: These include "behavioral" skill sets that help teams amplify their values and create output that goes well beyond expectations.

Let's dig deeper into these two skill sets.

The Hard Skills: How to Deliver on Your Expectations

High-performance marketing organizations start with a maniacal focus on their customers. You may think your firm is focused on customers, but is it "customer-obsessed"? Forrester reported that only 8 percent of decision-makers classify their company as fully customer obsessed.[1] Jennifer Ross, senior research director for Forrester's CMO Strategies, states:

> In high-performing B2B marketing organizations, the marketing ecosystem revolves around a uniform organizational understanding of the company's target audiences. In the age of the customer, Forrester believes that B2B organizations will outperform competitors only when the customer is at the center of the company's entire operating model and all functions consistently deliver superior customer experiences. Companies that are customer-centric tend to have four identifying characteristics: customer-led, insights-driven, fast, and connected. These characteristics are evident at all levels of the organization—from the C-suite down to the individual. Every process design, technology built or bought, interaction, and employee contributes to a marketing organization's ability to deliver exceptional experiences for its customers.[2]

To create a high-performance marketing organization, you need to have a clear strategy that puts the customer at the center of everything. After defining that strategy, marketing leaders can put the data, infrastructure, governance, team, and cross-functional processes in place to achieve goals. Since the customer is at the center of the strategy, the organization needs to take a close look at all of the processes in place and ensure that there are frictionless hand-offs across organizational boundaries—including brand, digital, demand gen, sales, customer success, and other functions. Data is at the center of this—if you don't get the data and analytics infrastructure right, your organization will struggle. While this effort spans sales and customer success, in a performance marketing mindset, the marketing organization and CMO take center stage in uniting organizational silos.

As an example, what is the quality of your marketing database? Do you know who you're marketing to? Can you easily identify the key personas, industries, geographies, customers, partners, and prospects from your database? We've worked for several data analytics companies and their databases always needed work. Spend the time to get it right—it will make your life easier in the long run!

Follow these steps to develop a high-performance marketing culture:

1. **Create a Customer-Obsessed Strategy**: Communicate it often so that every person within the company understands the strategy and their role in supporting and impacting it.

2. **Focus on Data Analytics Infrastructure and Ensure the Organization Is Data Literate**: If you cannot anticipate customer demands across multiple channels, your organization will struggle to meet customers where they are with the right experiences.

3. **Ensure a Modern Marketing Infrastructure**: In addition to the data and analytics infrastructure, you will need to put the right MarTech stack in place to support goals.

4. **Lead Cross-Functional Alignment**: The marketing leader should work extra hard to ensure that there is not only alignment between various marketing teams and channels but also alignment across marketing, sales, product, customer success, and partner ecosystems.

5. **Design Frictionless Hand-Offs**: As part of alignment, make sure there are frictionless hand-offs and orchestrate and automate processes across all of the different systems in place.

6. **Hire and Create an Engaged, Empowered Workforce**: Without the right organizational structure and an engaged workforce, you'll be in trouble. Make sure you hire, retain, upskill, and reskill the individuals in the organization for maximum impact.

7. **Avoid a "Yes Sir" Mentality**: Ensure people feel empowered to question and engage in healthy debate. This is good for the organization. Just be sure to be clear about when it's time to disagree and commit.

8. **Create a Culture of Experimentation**: Allow your teams to constantly innovate and experiment. Buying habits are constantly changing; marketing is ever-evolving. Learn from failures, celebrate successes, and constantly test and learn.

9. **Demand Operational Excellence**: Like a factory, the marketing organization should have an unceasing focus on operational excellence across all dimensions. For example, if you host a webinar, atomize the content and create several derivative pieces for further activation and amplification in the market. There should be standardized work processes and a BOM for all of the marketing functions.

Now that we understand that high-performance marketing is centered around customers and how to build a high-performance culture, let's look at why this is important.

The Soft Skills: Delivering Above and Beyond Expectations

Think Big, Start Small, Act Fast

In our careers, we have seen—and have been a part of—high-performing organizations. We have seen a few that have lost their way. For those, there often was not a common vision for the marketing team. There were competing visions. Brand marketing simply wanted to do more thought leadership. Demand gen wanted to gate every piece of content to drive pipeline. The inside sales team was calling prospects just to hit its numbers (not its fault, as it was not properly enabled).

For an organization to be effective, there needs to be a common vision across all aspects of it. This takes a strong leader who has a solid partnership with both the sales and product organizations.

The entire team needs to agree on a common set of objectives and key results (OKRs) and embark on a relentless journey to communicate this vision—the key priorities and initiatives across the entire organization.

There needs to be a steady drumbeat of communications to ensure that every person within the company understands the priorities and how their role impacts and aligns with them. In our experience, most of the marketing OKRs do a great job with demand gen metrics (often number one on the list) and brand and thought leadership, but often neglect any mention of sales enablement.

Part of the art of this kind of big thinking is to not have such a grandiose vision that it seems impossible to achieve. The leadership team must put together a logical sequence for how the organization is to achieve its goals. And it can't take too long to implement. It should be able to be implemented immediately, its evolution easy to understand, and fast acting. Start today.

Produce Something Rather Than Nothing

This brings us to our second characteristic of high-performance marketing teams. As General George Patton said: "A good plan violently executed *now* is better than a perfect plan next week."

We have seen many teams get bogged down in planning. Our top recommendation? Start doing something now.

Don't sacrifice getting something done for the sake of perfection. We have seen organizations spend an inordinate amount of time approving every piece of content—from whitepapers to web copy to ad copy. We're not advocating sloppy work, but are arguing that you need to empower the team to make decisions. In the digital age test and learn cycles should be focused on—being agile, if you will.

If the copy on a website or ad is not hitting the mark—change it tomorrow. We've seen many organizations treat some copy like it's being chiseled in stone, soon to be immutable. Yo, it's digital. If it's not effective, change it tomorrow! When an organization has too many review and approval processes, it can have a detrimental impact on the team. Members lose morale because all of their hard work simply gets redlined. The best leaders offer advice and recommendations to empower and build trust.

For whatever reason, marketing is one of the only jobs within an organization that everyone thinks they are qualified to do. Everyone has an opinion on the words, look, feel, and colors. This is fine, but companies ultimately can't be run by committee.

You Miss Every Shot You Don't Take

Take risks, lots of them. As mentioned in the previous section, we have been in some organizations that require extensive review and approval cycles. This will kill the soul of your marketing organization. A culture needs to be built that is open to new ways of operating, new ways of thinking, and new ways of doing things. Your workforce needs to have a growth mindset. Your group needs to take on challenges, learn from them, optimize, and refine for the next challenge. There are many articles and books on creating cultures of innovation with these recommended steps being common:

1. Empower Employees

2. Create a Culture of Learning and Upskilling

3. Lead and Adapt to Change Quickly

4. Provide Constructive and Frequent Feedback

5. Encourage Open Communications

Do whatever you can to create an innovation culture. Take risks. Reward the risk-takers. Your organization's most valuable asset is its workforce. If you can harness its potential, you will achieve amazing things.

Whatever You Do, Be Impactful

In our busy work worlds, we often get tunnel vision—email always needs to be checked, too many back-to-back meetings attended, and a bunch of busy work executed. It's easy to say yes to new tasks—much harder to say no. But we need to say no more often.

We've often had employees ask what they should be working on next (beyond their current deliverables). They understand the priorities. They know the business. They know what needs to be done. We frequently say the same thing: "You understand the priorities, and you are the expert. Whatever you do, do it, and be impactful."

Allow employees the freedom to explore and work on things that they enjoy. Don't overburden them with prescriptive to-do lists.

Clarity Through Action

As they say, leaders lead from the front. The best leaders don't sit back and direct from afar. They roll up their sleeves and participate in the process. Another famous George Patton quote: "Do everything you ask of those you command."

Nothing sets the bar higher than action. The best leaders and marketers get things done.

Passion, Skill, Knowledge (In That Sequence)

When looking to staff a high-performance marketing team, we recommend looking for individuals who are passionate about a subject or area and have skills and knowledge in a particular domain. You can always teach skills on the job, but passion can't be coached or taught. And it's the most important attribute to look for.

Learn Everyday: You Are Always a Novice

The best marketers we have worked with—and for—are continuous learners. They are not "know-it-alls." They have a natural curiosity about the world. They may be into music, acrobatics, exercise, reading, cooking, and a host of other hobbies. It all boils down to one thing—they like to learn about things.

Have Fun

In any work environment, it's always important to remember to have fun. It can be a little more challenging in a remote work environment, but it can be done. A team that has fun together grows stronger and will perform at a higher level.

In our current roles, we have a meeting series where we have a different theme every week—hat day, Hawaiian shirt day, rep your college day, outdoors day, and so forth. It's fun. We take time to ask about each other's backgrounds or costumes. You won't believe how many people want to get invited to this particular meeting. They see the social posts and want to be a part of it. This is one of the only meetings where no one is late, ever. If they are, they miss being in the picture.

Another recurring meeting features 80s music videos as people join (wow, the 80s were some crazy times). It gives people something to talk about and helps bind our 100 percent distributed team.

Practical Advice and Next Steps

- Use the templates we've provided to help begin or improve your marketing journey.
- Share feedback and experiences with us so we can improve our book.

Summary

As an African proverb states, "If you want to go fast, go alone. If you want to go far, go together." In marketing, it is the team that has the most success.

We hope our book has provided some practical tips, advice, best practices, and stories from the front lines of the B2B marketing world.

Please contact us. We'd love to hear from you.

Chapter 9 References

[1] Wizdo, Lori, Amy Bills, Barbara Winters, and Fiona Swerdlow. "The Customer Lifecycle Is the Design Muse to Accelerate Your Journey to Customer Obsession." Forrester. June 29, 2022. https://www.forrester.com/blogs/the-customer-lifecycle-is-the-design-muse-to-accelerate-your-journey-to-customer-obsession/.

[2] Ellett, John. "Building a High-Performance Marketing Team Is More Critical Now than Ever for B2B CMOs." Forbes. August 3, 2022. https://www.forbes.com/sites/johnellett/2022/08/03/building-a-high-performance-marketing-team-is-more-critical-now-than-ever-for-b2b-cmos/?sh=14e3adae356f.

Acknowledgments

Writing a book is a labor of love, a test of your patience, and perhaps a test of your sanity. We would like to thank our family, friends, colleagues, coworkers, and all those who have helped us along this journey for their support and encouragement.

To my (David's) wife Erin, thank you for putting up with the long hours and random questions with patience. Thank you to my sons Andy and Chris for their curiosity. And to my dog Brady, thank you for barking along the way.

To my (Kalyan's) family, thanks to Meera, Devya, and Viveka for believing that I can—and should—write a book and to my parents for teaching me to always strive to be better. And finally, to my co-author David, who helped turn a germ of an idea into a real finished product.

A big shout out to Namoi Miller, Mary Kern, and Robert Eve for their extensive peer review and feedback on early drafts. Their insights and suggestions have strengthened this book.

Thank you to Shawn Rogers, Rupa Menon, and Darrin Shimizu for agreeing to the interviews that appear throughout this book.

We would like to thank Bruno Trimouille, Lori Witzell, and Matthew Magne for the candid discussions on marketing curriculum, sports marketing sponsorships, and thought leadership programs.

We would like to thank Josipa Ćaran Šafradin for another beautiful cover design. They say don't judge a book by its cover, but people should judge this book by its cover because it's absolutely amazing. The design system we created in the first TinyTechGuide works fantastically!

To Taylor Porter and Peter Letzelter-Smith for the fine editing, proofreading, and indexing. The book is clearer, more readable, and interpretable.

Lastly, thank you to Thomas Been, Shawn Rogers, and Mary Kern for writing amazing endorsements for the book.

Remember, it's not the tech that's tiny, just the book!™

Ever onward!

About the Authors

David Sweenor is a top-25 analytics thought leader and influencer, international speaker, and acclaimed author who holds several patents. He is a marketing leader, analytics practitioner, and specialist in the business application of AI, ML, data science, the IoT, and business intelligence.

With over 25 years of hands-on business analytics experience, Sweenor has supported such organizations as Alteryx, TIBCO, SAS, IBM, Dell, and Quest in advanced analytic roles.

Follow David on Twitter (@DavidSweenor) and connect with him on LinkedIn (https://www.linkedin.com/in/davidsweenor/).

Kalyan Ramanathan is a revenue-focused marketer with more than 25 years of experience in go-to-market software and a deep understanding of SaaS/cloud-based IT, security, and analytics markets.

Kalyan has led marketing teams at leading companies like Alteryx, Sumo Logic, AppDynamics/Cisco, Crittercism/VMware, Opsware/HP, and others. Kalyan began his career at Intel and has an MBA from Stanford.

Follow Kalyan on Twitter (@kalyanAtWork) and connect with him on LinkedIn (https://www.linkedin.com/in/kalyanramanathan/).

Index

138, 146, 149

email, 52, 86, 91, 93, 100, 111,
118, 120, 127, 131, 135,
139, 150

field, 17, 18, 22, 25, 30, 87, 105,
106, 139

industry, 6, 16, 17, 18, 19, 20,
21, 22, 24, 25, 26, 28, 31,
45, 60, 62, 63, 65, 68, 70,
76, 78, 82, 88, 97, 121,
136, 142

influencer, 1, 25, 41, 76, 88, 96,
157

Integrated, 6, 9, 11, 12, 16, 19,
25, 33, 95, 96, 105, 106,
120

modern, iii, 2, 3, 7, 8, 75, 108,
114, 115, 127

partner, 15, 16, 18, 25, 31, 64,
88, 95, 97, 98, 101, 106,
115, 130, 147

partner ecosystem, 16, 18, 25,
31

plan, 23, 25, 26, 33, 35, 49, 67,
95, 96, 98, 99, 119, 120,
133, 135, 149

product, 3, 4, 5, 7, 9, 10, 11, 12,
15, 16, 17, 18, 19, 20, 21,
22, 23, 24, 25, 26, 28, 29,
30, 31, 33, 34, 35, 36, 38,
42, 44, 45, 49, 61, 67, 68,
69, 73, 76, 77, 78, 80, 86,
90, 91, 94, 95, 97, 98, 100,
103, 108, 110, 111, 119,
139, 147, 148, 155

software, 2, 3, 5, 6, 7, 10, 22, 29,
41, 43, 44, 45, 46, 47, 53,
57, 61, 62, 69, 81, 86, 89,
108, 111, 112, 129, 141,
157

solution, 5, 9, 10, 16, 18, 20, 25,
30, 31, 43, 49, 86, 93, 94,
96, 97, 98, 119, 139

technical, 16, 18, 20, 96, 132

marketing-originated bookings
(MOBs), 119

marketing technology (MarTech),
132

merger and acquisitions (M&A),
65

messaging guides, 83

mutually exclusive, collectively
exhaustive (MECE), 31

N

new product introduction (NPI),
33

O

objectives and key results
(OKRs), 149

onboarding, 86, 129

P

paid media, 93, 119, 121

Payment Card Industry (PCI),
133

pay-per-click (PPC), 102

personas, 1, 16, 20, 23, 24, 26, 28,
29, 33, 38, 77, 78, 96, 97, 98,
99, 100, 129, 147

pipeline, 36, 50, 55, 94, 97, 99,
103, 106, 114, 115, 119, 120,
121, 122, 123, 124, 133, 135,
139, 140, 141, 142, 148
  influenced, 73, 115, 122
  marketing-sourced, 122
  sourced, 115, 122

pipeline contribution, 99, 139,
140

pitch deck, 16

plays, 86, 94, 95, 97, 98, 100, 101,
122, 124, 127

point of view (POV), 73, 79

portfolio, 4, 10, 15, 16, 17, 18, 19,
20, 22, 23, 24, 25, 26, 29, 33,

Made in the USA
Las Vegas, NV
29 November 2023

81524455R00105